D1373489

Duquesne Studies

LANGUAGE AND LITERATURE SERIES

[VOLUME EIGHT]

GENERAL EDITOR:

Albert C. Labriola, *Department of English, Duquesne University*

ADVISORY EDITOR:

Foster Provost, *Department of English, Duquesne University*

PARADISE REGAIN'D

Paradise Regain'd

WORTHY T'HAVE NOT REMAIN'D SO LONG UNSUNG

---

by *John T. Shawcross*

DUQUESNE UNIVERSITY PRESS
Pittsburgh, PA

Published in the United States of America
by Duquesne University Press
600 Forbes Avenue, Pittsburgh, PA 15282

First Edition

Library of Congress Cataloging-in-Publication Data

Shawcross, John T.
Paradise regain'd.

(Duquesne studies. Language and literature series; v. 8)
Bibliography: p.
Includes index.
1. Milton, John, 1608–1674. Paradise regained.
I. Title. II. Series.
PR3565.S53   1988   821'.4   87–32945
ISBN 0–8207–0225–0

Contents

Acknowledgments

Parts of chapters 4 and 5 appeared in "The Structure and Myth of *Paradise Regain'd*," in *The Laurel Bough*, ed. G. Nageswara Rao (Delhi: Blackie and Son, 1982), pp. 1–14B. Parts of chapters 7 and 8 appeared in "The Genres of *Paradise Regain'd* and *Samson Agonistes*: The Wisdom of Their Joint Publication," in *Composite Orders: The Genres of Milton's Last Poems*, ed. Richard S. Ide and Joseph A. Wittreich, a special issue of *Milton Studies* 17 (1983): 225–48. All four chapters have been fully revised and are basically new.

I thank the University of Kentucky for a sabbatical leave which enabled me to employ time unencumbered by most of the duties of academic life to write this book.

Chapter One

Introduction

IN *The Heroic Argument: A Study of Milton's Heroic Poetry* (Madras: Macmillan and Co., 1971), M. V. Rama Sarma cogently argued that heroism for John Milton is predicated in "the view that blessed is the man who endures temptation, for when he is tried he receives the crown of life" (p. 134). In *Paradise Regain'd* "the Son of God . . . belongs to the category of 'patient or suffering heroes.' But such heroes who attain mastery over their passions and patiently endure all suffering and temptations are, according to Milton, more heroic than the ones who fight on the battlefield" (p. 154). Implied is the metaphor of life as a battlefield between forces of evil and its victims; and the further implication that life is not only a stage or theater on which the battle is fought, but a wasteland benighted by evil and the darkness of ignorance of "the crown of life." The brief epic, seen thus, becomes a mythic construct depicting a human's ideal passage through life to salvation: any human being like the Son must first gain "self-knowledge or awareness of divine similitude . . . through a gradual process" (p. 148), and, as a product of humankind, male and female, Man must take on the power of the father (the eagle) and the meekness of the mother (the dove). "Meekness" as in the beatitude of Jesus (Matt. 5:5) does not mean simply submissiveness (as to the will of Heaven) but gentleness, humbleness, patience, and a lack of resentment toward others' hate. The power of the mythic father is needed to defeat the

1

forces of evil on the battlefield; the meekness—mercy, love—of
the mythic mother is needed to achieve *caritas* or *agape*. Only
thus will the human being be able to follow the new com-
mandment "that ye love one another; as I have loved you,
that ye also love one another" (John 13:34). The fusion of
father and mother is the means to achieve heroic argument.

But further, Man must exhibit his humanness (the profane)
in conjunction with the sense of the divine within him (the
sacred), for as Milton counseled himself, and us, "All is, if I
have grace to use it so,/As ever in my great task-maisters eye"
(Sonnet 7). Such texts as "know ye not that your body is the
temple of the Holy Ghost which is in you" (1 Cor. 6:19)
underlie so much thought concerning the sacred and the
profane and humankind's theological concepts. For Carl
Jung, "The future indwelling of the Holy Ghost in man
amounts to a continuing incarnation of God. Christ, as the
begotten son of God and pre-existing mediator, is a first-born
and a divine paradigm which will be followed by further
incarnations of the Holy Ghost in the empirical man."[1] The
story of Jesus as the Son of God in the temptation in the
wilderness (where wilderness is a metaphor for life itself as in
Milton's *A Mask* and Dante's opening lines of the *Inferno*)
unites these concepts, even though the Son has undergone
kenosis (a complete emptying of himself as godhead; see Phil.
2:6–8). As Michael Lieb concludes, "From the theophanic
point of view, *Paradise Regain'd* ends, then, not only in a
celebration of ὁ ἅδιος in his revealed splendor but in a
contrast between two categories essential to the poem's
meaning, sacred and profane."[2]

Paradise Regain'd was reportedly Milton's favorite poem,
even being preferred to the grand, diffuse epic *Paradise Lost*.
While the latter work offers consolation that the fall of the
grandparents of humankind, Adam and Eve, can be seen as a

1. Carl Jung, *Answer to Job*, trans. R. F. C. Hull (Princeton: Princeton University Press, 1958 [1973]), Bollingen Series 20, p. 70.
2. Michael Lieb, *Poetics of the Holy: A Reading of Paradise Lost* (Chapel Hill: University of North Carolina Press, 1981), p. 73.

fortunate fall in that without it humankind would have been subject to future fall but, now fallen, can develop a "Paradise within, happier farr," it also indicates that true heroism is that which derives from the internal, not that exhibited on battle-fields for the gaining of power over one group or another. The "Paradise . . . happier farr" was to be achieved through "suffering for Truths sake," which "Is fortitude to highest victorie." Adding deeds to such knowledge, and faith, virtue, patience, temperance, and especially love, will allow one to possess that happier paradise. This message encased in the actions of the Son in *Paradise Lost* and enunciated by Adam and Michael at the end of the poem is made explicit in the brief epic as the Son, now incarnated as man, foils all the temptations of this world. He has suffered (and in the Passion will suffer more) for Truth's sake; he shows faith, virtue, patience, temperance. His deeds are deeds of obedience, which thus reverse the deed of disobedience recounted in *Paradise Lost*: Eve, through fraud, eats of the tree of forbidden knowledge; Adam, undeceived, partakes out of love for Eve, which, however, turns on narcissistic language, "Bone of my Bone, Flesh of my Flesh." The love of God the Father which the Son exhibits engages a positive relationship, the Son giving himself up to the guidance of the Father out of love of the Father. The parodic parallel of Satan as father figure and Sin as offspring is clear. Adam, however, does not maintain the figure of "father" as source out of which Eve was created, but rather succumbs to love of self.

The concepts of the briefer poem and its hopefulness for humankind surely furnish a basis for Milton's judgment about his poem. The clearer message for readers, since the message of *Paradise Lost* was undiscovered in Milton's own time by ordinary readers like Thomas Ellwood, and more disastrously escaped John Dryden, onward, in the misreading of Satan as hero and Milton as of his party, must have influenced the opinion reported by Milton's nephew Edward Phillips. The eighteenth century knew that opinion well, almost always dismissing it with amazement. But these concepts define Milton's theological position concerning the godhead and faith, the means to salvation, and individualistic rather than church-related action. Milton's "religion of one" and his removal of himself from church attendance and church contexts are logical adjuncts to the concepts of the briefer poem. Linked with the concepts of *The Tenure of Kings and Magistrates*, his message becomes twofold and politically powerful: the external war must be fought to defeat the perverters of truth, but the only full and lasting victory can come through individual internal armor. There is no retreat from the battlefield of life: one must sally forth and meet and defeat the Adversary. Humankind cannot take solace in escape, nor in rationalization amidst the scars of battle. The only means of defeating the Adversary is internal imperviousness to his wiles.

The Adversary of life is Satan (whose name, etymologically, in Hebrew means "adversary," deriving from a verb meaning "to attack" or "to accuse") or his images.[3] The Father's first reference to this major character of *Paradise Regain'd*, talking of the descent of the Spirit to Jesus at his baptism which pronounces him the Father's beloved Son, is:

That heard the Adversary, who roving still
About the world, at that assembly fam'd
Would not be last.   (I.33–35)

He is the Satan in Job, who has been "going to and fro in the earth, and . . . walking up and down in it" (Job 1:7). That very important book of the Bible is throughout an intertext for

---

3. A reader of Milton's prose, aware of this etymology, will find in the frequent citations of an adversary a residue of connotation suggesting the satanic; for example, in *Doctrine and Discipline of Divorce* we read, "For what less indignity were this [protection of public authority], then as if Justice her self the Queen of vertues, descending from her scepter'd royalty, instead of conquering, should compound and treat with sin her eternal adversary and rebel, upon ignoble terms" (*Complete Prose Works of John Milton*, ed. Lowell Coolidge [New Haven: Yale University Press, 1959], vol. 2, p. 323); or in *Of True Religion*, "But if they who dissent in matters not essential in belief, while the common adversary [specifically the Roman Catholic church] is in the field, shall stand jarring and pelting at one another, they will be soon routed and subdued" (*Complete Works of John Milton*, ed. Keith W. F. Stavely [New Haven: Yale University Press, 1982], vol. 8, p. 436). Hereafter reference will be Yale Prose for this edition.

Milton's poem, manifesting the parallel of the two narratives for Milton and many other Christians. Job is alluded to or cited frequently in *Paradise Regain'd* (see note 19 to chapter 2) and in other works (see note 18 to chapter 2). An understanding of Job and the biblical book is incumbent upon a full, perceptive reading of Milton's poem.

Almost the first biblical appearance of Satan is in Job 1:6ff., where he serves as a legal prosecutor within the heavenly court. This adversarial role is likewise his function in the other Old Testament texts in which he appears, 1 Chronicles 21:1, Psalm 109:6, and Zechariah 3:1–2. Satan is among "the sons of God"; he has been "going to and fro in the earth, and . . . walking up and down in it." The Lord's boast of Job as one unlike all other humans, "a perfect and an upright man, one that feareth God, and escheweth evil," is countered by Satan's challenge. "Doth Job fear God for nought? Hast not thou made a hedge about him, and about his house, and about all that he hath on every side? thou hast blessed the work of his hands, and his substance is increased in the land. But put forth thine hand now, and touch all that he hath, and he will curse thee to thy face." The Lord accepts the challenge and allows Satan to harass Job however he can, without interference from the Lord to alleviate such trial: "Behold, all that he hath is in thy power; only upon himself put not forth thine hand."

The effect of Satan in these writings, as indeed in *Paradise Regain'd*, is to compel a reader to the necessity of seeking understanding of God and God's way through revelation and relationship. Thus seen, Satan becomes a kind of emancipator for God by prospering good in humankind's relationship with God as the only counteraction to evil.[4] In Job 18 Harold Fisch sees "a hint of the ultimate fate of Satan as a prelude to the far-off divine event to which the whole creation was moving."[5]

4. Compare John S. Tanner's examination in "Job and the Prophets," *Cithara* 26(1986): 23–35.
5. Harold Fisch, "Creation in Reverse: The Book of Job and *Paradise Lost*," in *Milton and Scriptural Tradition: The Bible into Poetry*, ed. James H. Sims and Leland Ryken (Columbia: University of Missouri Press, 1984), p. 116.

In *Paradise Regain'd* we recognize, for Milton, the way that
far-off divine event can constantly and individualistically be
reached in this our life. Milton in no way castigates God the
Father in his references to Job as Jung does, but *Paradise
Regain'd* does nevertheless sustain Jung's concern: "the way in
which a modern man with a Christian education and back-
ground comes to terms with the divine darkness which is
unveiled in the Book of Job, and what effect it has on him."[6]
Looking at the positive view of Job and not at the negative
dimension of the Lord in that book of the Bible,[7] Milton
reworks the trials and oppression of the man Job by present-
ing the fundamental ways in which man may be diverted from
faith in God and come to desire the material and relief from
trial. The storm to which Jesus is subjected, an addition to the
Gospel account of the temptations, is Milton's means to
symbolize the satanic plagues upon Job. *Paradise Regain'd*
presents another "perfect and upright man" who "escheweth
evil," but one who is such through love rather than fear. "The
real reason for God's becoming man," Jung argued (p. 35),
"is to be sought in his encounter with Job," and "the immedi-
ate cause of the incarnation lies in Job's elevation," which he
sees as the victory of the vanquished and oppressed raising
one morally higher than God (pp. 42–44). The world-shaking
transformation of God into man, the *peripeteia* in the unfolding
of human life which the incarnation creates, lays forth that
"without which no higher level of consciousness can be
reached" (p. 44). For Milton, then, his task was to make clear
how the experience of the Son leads man to allow "the
Paraclete, the 'spirit of truth,' to dwell and work in individual
human beings, so as to remind them of Christ's teachings and
lead them into the light" (p. 71). Similar is Hart Crane's *The*

6. Jung, *Answer to Job*, p. 3. Revisionist Jewish thought that cannot encompass the
darkness of the godhead seen in the Holocaust is a directly opposite position to the
Christian rationalization of what appears to be the godhead's dual nature.
    7. Jung talks of "Yahweh's dual nature [which] has been revealed, and somebody
or something has seen and registered this fact. Such a revelation, whether it reached
man's consciousness or not, could not fail to have far-reaching consequences," ibid.,
p. 24. "[T]he atonement [is] not . . . the payment of a human debt to God,
but . . . reparation for a wrong done by God to man," p. 56.

Bridge, which employs as epigraph the verse from Job 1:7, in which external reality is made to become a part of the life of imagination: "the universal vision that Crane presents . . . is the saving grace of love which can not be fully realized until one has come to grips with and subdued the imponderable dinosaur of 'accepted multitudes.'"[8]

Such an immense theme as *Paradise Regain'd* presents is overwhelming, and, successful, it offers clear reason for Milton's preference of it to a theme of cause and effect,[9] but that theme of cause and effect as in *Paradise Lost* has submerged the message of *Paradise Regain'd* for his readers. Unlike Jung reading Job, readers of Milton's poem "have been taught to restrain doubt, to wait in patience the moment decreed by God," which "depends neither on 'Occasions's forelock' nor on the temporal flux of beginning, middle, and end. . . ."[10]

Yet a very specific problem has long bothered me about Milton's brief epic: Why is there such a major break between books I and II with a new induction and start in Book II? Barbara K. Lewalski, building upon the work of Elizabeth Pope, has demonstrated the theological structure of the poem.[11] This structure nullifies or answers certain questions of the past, though not the aforementioned problem. This present book argues that the answer lies in both the original conception of the literary work and its form, and the later reworking of that original conception to establish mythic intentions and meanings.

In this volume I explore these matters or implications: the

8. See my essay, "Influence for the Worse? Hart Crane Rethinks Milton," *The Visionary Company* 1–2 (1982): 78.

9. I explore the structural significance of cause and effect for the longer epic in *With Mortal Voice: The Creation of Paradise Lost* (Lexington: University Press of Kentucky, 1982), pp. 43–45.

10. The words are Edward W. Tayler's concluding his excellent chapter on the play of impatience and patience in this poem; see *Milton's Poetry: Its Development in Time* (Pittsburgh: Duquesne University Press, 1979), p. 184.

11. See Barbara K. Lewalski, *Milton's Brief Epic: The Genre, Meaning, and Art of Paradise Regained* (Providence: Brown University Press, 1966); Elizabeth M. Pope, *Paradise Regained: the Tradition and the Poem* (Baltimore: Johns Hopkins Press, 1947. London; Russell and Russell, 1961); as well as Lewalski's article on the structure in *Studies in Philology* 57 (1960): 186–200.

structure that delineates the battlefield, the achievement of self-knowledge, and the power or energy to be victorious on that battlefield, and the mythic concept of the patient hero whereby the crown of life may be attained. The Son of *Paradise Regain'd* becomes both the man-God and the heroic exemplar, and the human protagonist in the drama of life. Milton's message is not simply that humankind should follow the exemplar, for mere imitation (were it truly possible) does not create a being truly heroic of self, but that humankind must internalize the heroism of the Son, becoming itself imbued with magnanimity and self-reliance through faith in God.

The poem has a historical context as well, and part of that context is its form and genre, its time of composition as we know it, and thus its relationship with external events out of which its thinking arose and out of which impinge its meanings for the author and the expected readers. The context also involves the poem's relationship with other works of the author and may suggest authorial intentionality. All of that points toward a poem that has not only an artistic dimension, and in this case a philosophic (religious and moral) dimension, but a political meaning as well.

Chapter Two

The Date of Composition

SOME years ago I argued, on the basis of prosodic statistics, that Milton may have begun to write his brief epic as drama after *Samson Agonistes* and before *Paradise Lost*, that it originally consisted of parts of books I, II, and IV, then not much later III, and that it was revised into epic by additions and changes sometime after 1665.[1] Here I would like to restate a few of the points that I advanced but that have been apparently misread. My first concern was to question the way in which Ants Oras had used prosodic statistics to corroborate the traditional dating of Milton's three major poems.[2] Accordingly, the reported statistics were Oras's rearranged (except in section 3), since one cannot call into doubt the use of statistics if one uses different bases. Not all the prosodic tests were accepted as significant, and some were considered less significant than others. (None, let it be noted, negated the conclusions offered.) Other tests—for example, the reversed foot (a trochee rather than an expected iamb)—bear out the prosodic development suggested. My one assumption that some prosodic techniques are developed as the author achieves sureness of his or her art has been questioned, apparently because it implies that some techniques are poetically

1. John T. Shawcross, "The Chronology of Milton's Major Poems," *PMLA* 76 (1961): 345–58.
2. In South Atlantic Modern Language Association, *Studies in Milton*, ed. J. Max Patrick (Gainesville: University of Florida Press, 1953), pp. 128–97.

superior to others. As a typical example, an important test
reported was the use of run-on lines, a stylistic development,
which, except for specific purposes and except for those writ-
ing in such units as the heroic couplet, is increasingly em-
ployed as the poet matures and achieves command of his
talent. Witness the writing of many "poetizers" (not those, of
course, who employ the line as unit). The poetry is end-
stopped with a thud, and a meaningless comma is appended
to most lines; rarely is there enjambment. One need compare
only Milton's increased use of run-on lines in rhymed verse,
which is so easily end-stopped, to see this development and, I
trust, to recognize the aesthetically evaluative conclusion.

We may compare the three English odes ("On Time,"
"Upon the Circumcision," and "At a Solemn Musick"),
written in rhyme but not in definite patterns or line lengths,
with sonnets 8–15, and these with sonnets 16–23, and all with
psalms 1–8. The odes, written somewhere between 1633 and
1637 (although I would argue a time closer to the latter) total
78 lines of which 32 are run-on,[3] or a percentage of 41.0.
Sonnets 8–15, written between 1642 and 1648, total 112 lines,
of which 42 are run-on, or a percentage of 37.5. Sonnets
16–23, written between 1652 and 1658, total 112 lines, of
which 54 are run-on, or a percentage of 48.2. Psalms 1–8 were
paraphrased in various kinds of metric patterns in August
1653; they contain 262 lines, of which 153 are run-on,[4] or a
percentage of 58.4. The sonnet form makes the incidence of
run-on lines less frequent than in blank verse or nonstanzaic
forms.[5] The low percentage of run-on lines in sonnets 8–15

3. I use Oras's criterion: those lines that have no punctuation at the end of the
line are considered run-on. I report statistics from the 1673 printing of *Poems*, except
for sonnets 15, 16, 17, and 22, for which I use the copies in the Trinity MS, the first in
Milton's hand, the next two in a scribal hand (perhaps John Phillips's), and the last
in another scribal hand (perhaps Cyriack Skinner's). Certainly there may be discrep-
ancies between manuscript and print in such matters as punctuation, and Oras's
criterion is thus not reliable.

4. Omitted are Psalms 3:23; 6:18; and 8:8, which show no punctuation but which
clearly are strongly stopped. I have also not counted Sonnet 17, ll. 8, 12, 13; these
lines likewise have no punctuation though they should.

5. The differences between Sonnets 16–23 and Psalms 1–8, and their dates,
evidence this point. The psalms were clearly experimental of prosodic form and
meter; they show a high incidence, for example, of the reversed foot.

may thus owe that statistic to the influence of the sonnet form, which Milton in his later sonnets was to alter by changing the position of the *volta* (or turn) and, I think all critics will agree, by a purposeful increase in enjambment. But if we separate sonnets 8–15 into two groups, 8–11 (that is, "I did but prompt"), dated 1642–45/6, and 12–15, dated 1646–48, we find that the first group (56 lines) has 18 run-on lines, or 32.1 percent,[6] and the second group (56 lines) has 24 run-on lines, or 42.9 percent. Arranged in ascending order with Oras's statistics for *Comus* and the three major poems, we have:

Sonnets 8–11	32.1
Comus	39.9
Odes	41.0
Samson Agonistes	42.1
Sonnets 12–15	42.9
Paradise Regain'd	45.2
Sonnets 16–23	48.2
Psalms 1–8	58.4
Paradise Lost	58.8 [7]

Acknowledging the lesser frequency of run-on lines in rhymed verse and even lesser frequency than that in such forms as the sonnet, we should be struck at the increase in run-on lines as we move from *Comus* (1634 through 1637) to the Odes (perhaps closer to 1637), to sonnets 12–15 (1646–48), to sonnets

6. With these four sonnets we have a clear case of unreliability of the criterion for run-on lines. The manuscript versions (No. 8 in an amanuensis's hand and the others in Milton's) show much less punctuation at the ends of lines than do the printed versions. A modern printing of these sonnets would see an increase in run-on lines to at least twenty–four, or 42.9 per cent. Compare particularly the punctuation of Sonnet 9 in the 1673 edition and in modernized versions.

7. Corroborative of my point are the stanzaic *The Passion*, written March 1630, which has 56 lines, including 11 run-on, or 19.7 percent, and Sonnets 1–7 plus *Canzone*, written in 1630–32, which have 113 lines, including 40 run-on, or 35.4 percent.

16–23 (1652–58), to psalms 1–8 (1653), to *Paradise Lost* (developed between 1640 and 1665).

This is but one test, of course, but it is an important one. The preceding strongly documents for all students of Milton that he did increase his use of run-on lines as time went by and his versification became more experienced and more experimental. The conclusion stares us in the face that Milton's verse (any verse, I should think) evidencing such controls must indeed be more mature than that that does not. A long poem, like *Paradise Lost*, written over a period of time, will naturally register differences in its various parts, and a single statistic as reported here will have been influenced by later revisions. The application of this conclusion to *Samson Agonistes* and *Paradise Regain'd*, a conclusion that is surely logical, leads to the clear-cut realization that the two works are earlier in composition than *Paradise Lost*, although parts or revisions may have been executed after composition of *Paradise Lost* was complete. The fact that these two are not in rhyme (except for a few instances in the dramatic poem) further underscores the significance of the lesser enjambment that one might have expected in unrhymed verse. My former argument concerning the composition of *Paradise Regain'd* contends that revisions after 1665 achieved epic form by relatively slight changes to indicate speakers and reactions, by slightly greater changes to move a few dramatic speeches into narrative form, and by the addition of various sections. The statistics for run-on lines cannot be used with a high degree of mathematical accuracy because of revisions, composition over a period of time for some of the works, and the affinities that rhyme and specific genre (the sonnet) may have for end stoppage, but certainly the general impression delivered by these statistics is that *Paradise Regain'd* was composed in large part prior to 1650.

The testimony of Thomas Ellwood about the composition of the brief epic, as well, can be developed further, and his words, taken with such dating as that suggested, lead to a conclusion different from that of tradition. In *The History of the Life of Thomas Ellwood* (London, 1714), we read: "but what hast thou to say of *Paradise found*? He made no Answer, but sate some time in a Muse: then brake of that Discourse and fell upon another Subject. After the Sickness was over, . . . he shewed me his Second POEM, called PARADISE REGAINED; and in a pleasant Tone said to me, *This is owing to you: for you put it into my Head, by the Question you put to me at Chalfont; which before I had not thought of*" (p. 234). Read afresh and without a preconception of the dates of *Paradise Lost* (shown to Ellwood around 1665) and *Paradise Regain'd*, these words indicate that when Milton "sate some time in a Muse," he was considering what he could create to contrast with his epic poem, a poem concerned with the way by which paradise is lost (that is, through disobedience). His breaking off that subject after a while may indicate that Milton conceived what he could create as contrast: an example of how the paradise within can be gained by obedience and faith. Harris F. Fletcher has pointed out that the concept of the salvation of man through obedience such as that exemplified by the Son was well woven into *Paradise Lost*:[8] see I.1–10; III.94–95, 107, 203–5; V.501, 512–14, 522, 536–37, 541, 611–12; VI.687, 902, 909–21; VII.159; VIII.25; XII.386–435. Fletcher concluded that "its construction is too sound, its composition too adroit to allow me to believe otherwise than that *Paradise Regained* was at least well developed in Milton's mind even before *Paradise Lost* was published."[9] Milton seems not to have thought long to come up with an answer to Ellwood's question; but he did not answer that what he had to say about "Paradise found" was already discernible in the manuscript Ellwood had read. I suggest that what he recalled while he "sate some time in a Muse" was instead his half-finished work on the Son's defeat of temptation through obedience and faith. His "muse" envisioned both the need to make the Son's example more explicit than it was to an average reader of *Paradise Lost* and the nature of the new work which would not only use material

---

8. Harris F. Fletcher, *John Milton's Complete Poetical Works* (Urbana: University of Illinois Press, 1948), vol. 4, p. 10. The first edition of *Paradise Regain'd* is here given in facsimile; volume one of this collection prints facsimiles of the Trinity MS poems and the 1673 edition of the shorter poems.

9. Ibid., p. 11.

already available but also cap his achievement in the long epic by a contrastive form, contrastive tone, and contrastive style, all appropriate to his subject and its prime mover, the Son.

Milton himself called *Paradise Regain'd* his "prompted Song" (I.12), but we, reading the line traditionally, assign the inspiration of the subject and its treatment to Ellwood. As it all happened, Ellwood could aggrandize to himself this creative honor, but we should be skeptical that this was indeed the fact. More logical, I believe, is a reading of Ellwood's words and Milton's reference to his "prompted Song" to mean Milton's remembrance of a discarded dramatic work which Ellwood's question indicated to Milton could be made into a significant contribution: the means to find paradise, or rather, regain paradise by an inward development of obedience because of faith, and faith because of love. Ellwood's question makes one aware that *Paradise Lost* would stress for the average reader the tragic dimension of Adam and Eve's losing Paradise. And, of course, many—most, I suppose—readers have seen the poem this way. They do not sense the comedic mode, nor do they see that the focus is *not* upon Book IX, and certainly they very frequently forget the role of the Son in the poem and the message he exemplifies—the same message that Milton lays quite bare in his brief epic. This misreading of the full poem that is *Paradise Lost* has created antagonisms toward the inclusion of books XI and XII and toward the nature of books V and VI, presenting the War in Heaven. The last two books have long been looked at as biblical history, which they are not really: they present selected types of followers of the faithless and the faithful; they offer the types of the Son in his offices as prophet, king, and priest; they offer examples of boldness and of meekness, of inhumanity toward humankind by humans, and of false war against the humanity of others and the proper war against the enemies of God. The War in Heaven and its preliminaries develop the same contrast, the comic activities of the rebellious angels being laughed at by God (in allusion to Psalm 2).

The date of *Paradise Regain'd* suggested by Ellwood's remarks places it after June (exact dates uncertain), when

Milton was staying at Chalfont St. Giles, Bucks, because of the plague in London. The completed *Paradise Lost* has accordingly been placed before this time—usually just before. How long a time elapsed between the conversation at Chalfont St. Giles and "After the Sickness was over" can only be guessed at. The second conversation Ellwood reports can date as early as late 1666, and the impression is that it took place at that time, that is, not long after the plague had left London. Perhaps at least it took place before mid-1669 when Milton apparently moved from Jewin Street to Artillery Walk, Bunhill Fields; Ellwood mentions only the Jewin Street residence. As I view the original composition of *Paradise Regain'd* to be before 1650, I conclude that in 1665–66, if Milton had his manuscripts with him at Chalfont St. Giles, or in 1666 through mid-1669, the original dramatic fragment received alterations and additions because of an epic shift prompted by Ellwood's question.

I think 1669 can be judged the *terminus ad quem* for the poem because of these conditions; this may receive corroboration from the questions surrounding its publication. All known copies of the volume give 1671 as the date of publication, but it was licensed on 2 July 1670 (*Term Catalogues* I.56) and scheduled to appear around 10 September, its date of registration (*Stationers' Register*, vol. 2, p. 415). The volume is listed in an advertisement for sale by John Starkey, the publisher, which would seem to have been made up around May 1670.[10] Anthony Wood and John Toland both call it a quarto and date it 1670 (known copies are octavos).[11] These "facts" have been known, but only recently did I point out that early catalogues of books at the Bodleian Library likewise list the volume with the date 1670. See *Catalogus Impressorum Librorum Bibliothecæ Bodlejanæ in Academia Oxoniensi. Cura & Opera Thomæ Hyde è Coll. Reginæ Oxon. Protobibliothecarii* (Oxonii: E Theatro Sheldoniano, 1674), p. 457, and *Catalogue Impressorum Librorum*

10. See J. Milton French, *The Life Records of John Milton* (New Brunswick: Rutgers University Press, 1954), vol. 5, pp. 26, 32, 96.

11. See Helen Darbishire, ed., *The Early Lives of Milton* (London: Constable, 1932), pp. 9, 46.

Bibliothecæ Bodleianæ in Academia Oxoniensi (Oxonii: E Theatro Sheldoniano, 1738), vol. 2, p. 182. The total disappearance of a copy of a 1670 printing is hard to believe; it is equally disturbing that these varied sources could all be in error about the date.

What this suggests for *Paradise Regain'd* and *Samson Agonistes* is that they were both completed as we know them before mid-1670. A date of new and total composition for both poems between mid-1665 and mid-1670 is not impossible, but it is perhaps to be treated skeptically. Without getting into the question of the date of the dramatic poem, we should note that it may have been added to *Paradise Regain'd* to fill up a rather slim volume, as Milton's prolusions were added to his familiar letters in 1674. The publication of *Accedence Commenc't Grammar* in 1669, of *The History of Britain* in 1670, of *Artis Logicæ Plenior Institutio* in 1672, of *Poems* in 1673 with the additions of the very early *Fair Infant Elegy, At a Vacation Exercise*, and *Apologus ad Rustico et Hero*, and of *Epistolarum Familiarium* in 1674, all attest to Milton's cleaning house and getting things written much earlier finally into print. Remaining to appear were only the State Papers and *Character of the Long Parliament*, which apparently created difficulties because of their political nature, *De doctrina christiana*, which seems to have suffered disregard because of the fate of the State Papers, and *A Brief History of Moscovia*, which may have been delayed because of its brevity. Of course, it would be *Paradise Regain'd* that would receive top billing in the volume, not only to capitalize upon the comparison with *Paradise Lost*, which had appeared in six issues during 1667–69, but to become part of a popular concern represented by such theological works as *The Key to Paradise, Opening the Gate to Eternal Salvation* (1675) and Henry Hare, Baron Coleraine's *The Situation of Paradise found out: Being an History of a Late Pilgrimage into the Holy Land* (1683).

The similarities that critics have found in these "companion" poems should be viewed in terms of Milton's total vision, not closeness of composition date; the dissimilarities, in terms of nonplanning of the works as companion pieces originally. William Riley Parker implies such dissimilarities when he writes, I believe quite wrongly: "To move, in the 1671 volume, from Book IV of *Paradise Regain'd* on to the Preface of *Samson Agonistes* is to encounter intellectual confusion."[12] I have discussed the wisdom of joint publication of the poems elsewhere, for I see one informing the other and together the poems offering the ideal and the actuality in the matter of humankind's salvation.[13] But their publication amidst the 1669–74 appearances of early works emboldens the argument for their earlier date of original composition.

Evidence of dating *Paradise Regain'd* has seldom been offered. All but one of the early biographers give slight notes based on publication dates. Aubrey has, "After he was blind he wrote these following Books viz. Paradise lost, Paradise regained, Grammar . . .,"[14] the last item exposing Aubrey's lack of knowledge, since *Accedence Commenc't Grammar* was compiled before Milton's blindness. Edward Phillips also indicates that he was not informed: *"Paradice regain'd,* which doubtless was begun and finisht and Printed after the other was publisht."[15] Only the so-called Anonymous Biographer (apparently Cyriack Skinner) has a significant comment: "Also the composing *Paradise Lost* and the framing a *Body of Divinity* out of the Bible: All which, notwithstanding the several Calamities befalling him in his fortunes, hee finish'd after the Restoration: As also the *Brittish* history down to the Conquest, *Paradise regaind, Samson Agonistes*, a Tragedy, *Logica & Accedence commenc'd Grammar* & had begun a *Greek Thesaurus.*"[16] "As also" can mean only "finish'd after the Restoration," an interpretation corroborated by the addition concerning the Greek thesaurus, only then *begun.* These items—and we know this to be true for the history, the logic,

12. William R. Parker, *Milton: A Biography* (Oxford: Clarendon Press, 1968), vol. 2, p. 1139.

13. John T. Shawcross, "The Genres of *Paradise Regain'd* and *Samson Agonistes*: The Wisdom of Their Joint Publication," in *Composite Orders: The Genres of Milton's Last Poems*, ed. Richard S. Ide and Joseph Wittreich, special issue of *Milton Studies*, 17, pp. 225–48. See also ch. 8 of this present volume.

14. Darbishire, *Early Lives*, p. 3.

15. Ibid., p. 75.

16. Ibid., p. 29.

and the grammar—were, Skinner tells us, *finished* after the Restoration, implying that they had been begun before 1660.

During middle 1641 through early 1642, Milton set down in the Trinity MS (pp. 40–41) possible dramatic subjects on the Passion of Christ, including as the last item in his manuscript notes a brief outline for "Christus patiens."[17] Since no subject on the temptation is recorded, we may infer that it recommended itself to Milton after early 1642, but we might suppose also that the trend of thought that hit upon the possibilities of the Passion led not too long afterward to the temptation. At least by 1649, as Fletcher noted (p. 9), Milton was concerned with the story of the temptation in the wilderness, for he refers to it in *The Tenure of Kings and Magistrates* (Columbia, V.16) and in *Defensio prima* (Columbia, VII.170), written during 1650. Likewise between 1642 and 1649 we see Milton repeatedly referring to the story of Job,[18] whose patience was to be a model for *Paradise Regain'd* and who was also to supply at least ten allusions.[19]

Another avenue into determining the date of original composition may be spelling. Analysis of orthography to date any of Milton's works involves thorny problems: textual interference from scribe and compositor prohibits easy conclusions, and, of course, revisions, additions, and the like which I

17. See my unpublished dissertation, "Milton's Spelling: Its Biographical and Critical Implications" (New York University, 1958), p. 200.

18. *The Reason of Church-Government* (noted as a brief model of an epic; Yale Prose, I [1953], 813), *Apology* (I.907), *Doctrine and Discipline of Divorce* (II [1959], 263, 277), *Tetrachordon* (II.590), *Colasterion* (II.728), *Eikonoklastes* (III [1962], 456, 484, 535). Before 1642 only one specific allusion seems to have been made ("On the Morning of Christs Nativity," 117–24), and I would add the pejorative use of "green" in Sonnet 9 (1643–45) to his remembrance of this book of the Bible (Job 8:12–13, 16). After 1649 three pamphlets cite Job; *Paradise Lost* contains a number of verbal references; and *De doctrina christiana* has 166 quotations or citations according to Harris F. Fletcher, *The Use of the Bible in Milton's Prose* (Urbana: University of Illinois Press, 1929), including the following from book 1, chapter 8 (Yale Prose, VI [1973]), "Good temptations are those which God uses to tempt even righteous men, in order to prove them. He does this not for his own sake—as if he did not know what sort of men they would turn out to be—but either to exercise or demonstrate their faith or patience, as in the case of Abraham and Job, . . ." (trans. John Carey).

19. Mentioned: I.147, 369, 425; III.64, 67, 95. Verbal allusions: I.33; II.416; IV. 455, 624.

see Milton making sometime after 1665 create major difficulties. Therefore, before we look at the text of *Paradise Regain'd*, let us see what happened to Sonnet 11, for which we have a text in Milton's hand, one in a scribe's hand, and one from its 1673 printing, and also to *The New Forcers of Conscience*, for which we have a text in a scribe's hand and its 1673 printing. Both must have been transcribed at least once more for the 1673 copy text,[20] and *New Forcers* may have existed in a copy in Milton's hand.

In the sonnet Milton does not write idle final *e* on uncompounded or uninflected words, but the scribe adds such *e*'s to: "theire," 1; "knowne," 2; "moone," 7; "pearle," 8; "freedome," 9; "meane," 11; "marke," 13; "roave," 13; "losse," 14. All were thus potential examples of spelling not in accord with Milton's practice.[21] In each case the *e* is omitted in 1673, either because it was not found in the copy set or, more likely, because the compositor simplified. It seems to have been the compositor who simplified such spelling in poems printed from his 1645 copy text (for example, in *Comus*, "pass," 79; "less," 88; "rudeness," 177; "unless," 266; "ear," 559). This may also account for the alteration of "set," 10, from "sett" (a scribal change). Since Milton's and the scribe's spelling "bawl," 9, became "bawle" in print, it is difficult to accept the intervention of a corrector-agent for Milton. The conclusion is fair that the spelling "bawle" occurred in the 1673 copy text because of some intermediary scribe and was thus set by the 1673 compositor contrary to his usual practice. The simplified "clogs," 1; "dogs," 4; "hogs," 8; and "frogs," 5, are repeated by the scribe, but the printed forms have two *g*'s. Is this the compositor's spelling or an intermediary scribe's? This too seems more likely to be traceable to that scribe. The following

20. Another copy of *New Forcers* was probably made in the 1650s in the now-lost inner leaf of the quarto sheets bound into the folio Trinity MS.

21. See Shawcross, "Milton's Spelling," and the following: "One Aspect of Milton's Spelling: Idle Final 'E,'" *PMLA* 78 (1963): 501–10; "What We Can Learn from Milton's Spelling," *Huntington Library Quarterly* 26 (1963): 351–61; and "Orthography and the Text of *Paradise Lost*" in *Language and Style in Milton*, ed. Ronald David Emma and John T. Shawcross (New York: Frederick Ungar, 1967), pp. 120–53.

changes from Milton's and his scribe's copies, however, may arise from either an intermediary scribe or the compositor: "antient," 4; "libertie," 4; "raild," 6; "progenie," 6; "sence-less," 9;[22] "libertie," 11. Next we should observe that in inflected forms Milton generally omitted *e*, but that the scribe made one change ("owles," 4), which continued into print.[23] Other spelling of the first scribe may lie behind the 1673 text: "their," 1, 9; "far," 13; and "roave," 13.[24] On the other hand, we can trace Milton's own spelling in the printed text: "strait," 3; "roav(e)," 13; "wast," 14.

From the textual evidence of Sonnet 11 we realize: (1) some spelling in the printed text may derive from Milton; (2) some spelling may derive from the scribe or scribes; (3) some spelling may derive from the compositor; and, most important, (4) no controls over text seem to have operated during the first scribal transcription, during the copy text transcription, or during printing. Further we see that elements of Milton's spelling may remain ("roav-"), though the final form was not his ("roave"), and that certain compositorial or scribal changes may have moved a spelling back to that which was coincident with Milton's.

Similar conclusions may be drawn from an analysis of the frequently "un-Miltonic" text of *New Forcers*. But a most important additional realization arises: an intermediary copy (apparently not one probably made in the 1650s by Milton's most careless and uninformed scribe who transcribed sonnets 11–14 and penned the Bradshaw letter in 1653) was prepared by someone aware of Milton's practices. Two significant changes from the Trinity MS copy are found in the printed version which would not have been created by the compositor: "wors," 14, and "wholsom," 16. Certain spellings ("vowes," 2; "seise," 3; and "hereticks," 11) suggest that the Trinity MS copy lies behind the printed text, and therefore we cannot

22. Milton: "senseles"; scribe: "sensles."

23. Milton's exceptional "hindes," 5, repeated by the scribe, appears without an *e* in print.

24. That the first scribe's copy was employed for the final text is seen in the word "cuckoes," 4; Milton's copy has "buzzards."

argue derivation of these two spellings from a lost copy in Milton's hand. The changes seem rather to result from an informed scribe, but one who did not fully "correct" his text.

Constantly remembering that some of the spelling in the first edition of *Paradise Regain'd* may derive from Milton (if indeed he himself put down sections of the poem first), from his scribe or scribes, and from the 1671 compositor, we can still conclude from the evidence that original composition of the brief epic may date before Milton's total blindness in very early 1652, probably before mid-1651 when he seems to have been functionally blind. Certainly the first seven lines as they now stand were written after *Paradise Lost* was published, and other lines and passages were added or altered (not only in terms of a revised versification). The argument that Milton painstakingly spelled out his text letter for letter to his scribe derives from a comment in the Latin letter to Peter Heimbach, dated 15 August 1666: "if you find anything incorrectly written down or not punctuated, you will impute it to the boy who has taken it from my dictation, being utterly ignorant of Latin, so that I was forced, while dictating, not without misery, to spell out each of the letters completely." It is farfetched to argue that he spelled out English to his scribe in the same way, although he certainly may have cautioned the scribe about specific words and in general trained him in the orthography of certain words or groups of words. Peculiar Miltonic spellings occur throughout the 1671 text of *Paradise Regain'd*, the only text of the poem that we have. These spellings include preteritive forms[25] and reflexive pronouns, and words that would not have resulted from a scribe's instructed practice or Milton's dictation; for example, "sirnam'd," "unsutable," "chuse," "terrases," "wholsom." No section of the poem shows orthography that could not have been Milton's, although there are sections which do not

---

25. Incidentally, "Regain'd" is the spelling of the first edition of the poem and agrees with Milton's practice. The mixture of spellings in this book records the lack of attention most Milton critics have given to this detail, although technically the apostrophized form yields two syllables and "Regained" yields three. See, for example, the significance for IV.608: "Temptation, hast regain'd lost Paradise."

contain peculiar spellings. Odd spellings, some containing "errors" in terms of what Milton would have written (based upon a full study of all holograph materials), conform with his practices.[26] Such a great number of agreements with Milton's practices point to the conclusion that his autograph lay behind the text in at least many sections of it. These data cannot all be ascribed to coincidence or some of the practices of the scribe or compositor.

The preceding implies composition before 1651. The consistent spelling "-less" and "-ness" limits either composition or rewriting to a date after middle 1646, but this consistency may result from the printer's normalization of the text, even though he is not always consistent in other examples. The extensive use of "-ic" suggests composition or rewriting after the middle of 1644, but there are a few examples of "-ick"; I have summarized these spellings in a table.

26. Selected odd spellings include: *Book I*: "e're," 1; "wast," 7; "highth," 13; "aw," 22; "facil," 51; "stroak," 59; "flowr," 67; "dores," 82; "wast," 104; "thir," 115; "raign," 125; "o're," 140; "sollicitations," 152; "entring," 174; "brest," 185; "persu'd." 195; "perswasion," 223; "highth," 231; "strait," 259; "thir," 501.

Book II: "expresly," 3; "thir," 9; "thir," 12; "thir," 29; "highth" and "thir," 45; "thir," 48; "gon," 116; "sollicitous," 120; "undergon," 132; "perswasion," 142; "thir," 148; "perswasive," 159; "brest," 167; "thir" (2), 176; "sirnam'd," 199; "thir," 235; "hungring," 244; "wandring," 246; "hungring," 259; "towring," 280; "wandring," 313; "thir," 371; "thir," 376; "highth" and "thir," 436; "o're," 478.

Book III: "battel," 20; "thir" (2), 55; "battels," 73; "thir," 78; "rowling," 86; "unsutable," 132; "thir," 143; "raign," 178; "raign," 216; "thir," 226; "thir," 237; "unadventrous," 243; "thir," 246; "spatious," 254; "strait," 256; "joyn'd" and "thir," 258; "fertil" and "oyl," 259; "towr'd," 261; "hunderd," 287; "hast," 303; "powr'd," 311; "thir," 313; "thir" and "battell," 322; "thir," 325; "Pioners," 330; "thir," 344; "chuse," 370; "thir," 379; "thir," 382; "battels," 392; "numbring," 410; "thir," 419; "Gentils," 425; "joyn'd," 426; "thir," 430; "thir," 432; "remembring," 434; "hast," 437; "thir," 439; "falshood," 443.

Book IV: "perswasive," 4; "spight," 12; "powr'd," 16; "battry," 20; "bredth," 27; "highth," 39; "terrases," 54; "entring," 62; "thir," 63; "thir," 65; "thir," 89; "thir," 114; "wast," 123; "thir," 136; "thir," 139; "thir," 141; "o're," 223; "thir," 231; "thir," 234; "flowrie," 247; "democratie," 269; "sirnam'd," 279; "waight," 282; "wearisom," 322; "thir" (2), 340; "thir," 342; "tasts," 347; "thir," 353; "thir," 355; "thir" and "stile," 359; "lowring," 398; "meer," 400; "thir," 414; "staid," 421; "thir" (State 2), 424; "grisly," 430; "wholsom," 458; "wastful," 461; "perfet," 468; "persue," 470; "swoln," 439; "meer," 535; "agen," 537; "thir," 557; "strook," 576; "strait," 581; "flowry," 586; "indu'd," 602; "e're," 621; "thir," 632.

Book	"-ic"	"-ick"	
I	4	2	"publick" 204; "tyrannick" 219
II	3	4	"majestick" 216; "publick" 52, 84, 465
III	4	0	
IV	22	1	"publick" 96

Is it possible that the first writing of the poem was before the middle of 1644? We might note "-ears" where Milton after 1646 would probably have written "-eares" (only one of this group uses the *e*—"turmes," IV.66); "-ays"; "sov'raign," I.84; "ruine," I.102; IV.413; "Hebrew," IV.336; "humane," I.221, 298, 308; II.137, 246 (apparently changed after middle 1642, perhaps 1643–44), but "human," III.231, 402; IV.265, 599; "mee," II.259; IV.486, 497.[27] These may come through because sections in which they are found were written in 1642–44. Since none of these "earlier" spellings (including "-ick") exist in Book III, it is possible that this book was written entirely after 1646. Perhaps, too, Book IV was revised or augmented more than books I and II, after 1646. There is a mixture of "-en" and "-'n" in all four books, with "-en" being more frequent. Notable here are the seventeen occurrences of "-en" in Book II, but only three of "-'n" ("fall'n," 31; "ris'n," 127; and "soft'n," 163). Book III gives six spellings with "-en" and two with "-'n." However, two of these Book III "-en" spellings require two syllables and the other four are "heaven," requiring one syllable. Perhaps Milton's "heavn" was normalized by the compositor.

My former suggestion and now the added conclusion on the basis of spelling data that the third book of *Paradise Regain'd* is basically later than the other three is borne out by and at the same time helps explain the problem of the temptations with

27. "Hee" is found at II.199, and IV.638; and "wo" at I.398, 399. These could be Milton's spellings although there is not a single example of "hee" in Milton's extant autograph, or the amanuensis's or the compositor's.

which each book of the poem is concerned. Elizabeth Pope discussed the three biblical temptations cited in Luke as gluttony or the flesh (*concupiscentia carnis*), vainglory or the world (*concupiscentia oculorum*), and avarice or the devil (*superbia vitæ*), and assigned them to Books I, II, and IV, respectively.[28] Book III deals with a specific identification rather than with the whole temptation motive. "For a poet actually working with the Luke order to identify the sin of Satan with *regna omnia mundi*," Pope wrote, "was certainly very much out of the ordinary" (p. 68).

The dating of Books I, II, and IV originally during 1642–44 (to 1646) suggests that at first Milton projected a shorter work concerned with the generalized and universal temptation motive. The dating of Book III during middle 1646–49 (and before 1651) indicates its interpolation into the Lucan scheme, and explains in part the lack of cohesiveness which commentators have noted. Such an addition as Book III seems to be indicates a lack of satisfaction with the work, for a while at least. This may account for its not being published until revised into epic sometime after 1665.

I therefore argue that the first draft of *Paradise Regain'd* could have been written in 1642–44, that it would then have been revised and reautographed in middle 1646–49, and that only revisions into epic were made for publication. Revision into epic would involve a different versification perhaps, a movement of "speeches" into narrative by addition of such speech tags as "To whom quick answer Satan thus return'd" (II.172)—most such speech tags constituting a full iambic line—or "To whom thus Jesus" (II.317); and the rendering of some speeches into narrative perhaps and the addition of narrative sections. There are few strictly narrative sections in the whole of the poem, many being brief passages or comment on the action, some being descriptive of action that production would have made clear or of changes of scene.

The topics for drama concerning Christ on p. 40 of the Trinity MS plans, written from middle 1641 through early

---

28. Pope, *Paradise Regained.*

1642, reflect Milton's first groping for a fit subject using the Son as central character. The brief outline for "Christus patiens," written in early 1642, shows development of one subject, which work continuing may have produced the embryonic *Paradise Regain'd* in dramatic form, although the plan here is entirely different from the eventual poem. (With the thinking about the Son as a central figure in a literary work and with the abandonment of this early writing sometime after 1650 or so, Milton may have decided to include the Son as a central character in what came to be *Paradise Lost*, which had early on shown no inclusion of the Son in that dramatic work. Some of the sections in the long epic, however, may have utilized other writing in which the Son may have figured strongly; for example, Book III.) Dramatic form may not have been eschewed until after *Samson Agonistes* was reworked, ca. 1647–48 (if we accept early initial composition of that dramatic poem and Parker's dating[29]). Thus, if the foregoing arguments are valid, *Paradise Regain'd* in a revised form and text, much of which remains in the extant version, is probably to be dated 1646–48. Any epical change is difficult to assign; but it probably did not take place until after the epic shift for *Paradise Lost*, which I would suggest was occurring in 1655–58 and which had occurred by 1660, at which times Milton returned to that poem. I thus would date the epic shift for what became *Paradise Regain'd* only after Milton "sate some time in a Muse," that is, after 1665. Considering all the circumstances of his personal life and of the publication (or pending publication) of other (though earlier) works in the five years 1665–70, with a possible narrowed dating from late 1665 to late 1666 according to Ellwood's remarks, it makes much more realistic sense for the production of *Paradise Regain'd* if Milton were revising an already worked-up manuscript than if he were starting quite fresh as a result of the amazingly imperceptive remarks of the gentle but not very creative Thomas Ellwood.

29. William Riley Parker, "The Date of *Samson Agonistes*," *Philological Quarterly* 28 (1949): 145–66. See also his extended discussion in *Milton: A Biography*, vol. 2, pp. 903–17.

If much writing of *Samson Agonistes* and *Paradise Regain'd* and
some of *Paradise Lost* is placed in the 1640s, what we have
thought accurate biographical knowledge will have to be
revised.[30] As far as one can reconstruct Milton's activities
between 1642 and 1649, besides his tutoring and studying, we
find quite a lot of "free" time, even though we maximize the
time spent on publications and assume that various activities
were not generally concurrent.

	Activities	Possible Free Time
1642	January: Finishing *Reason of Church-Government*	
		February
	March-April: Writing *An Apology*	
	May?: Marries	May-December
	July?: Wife returns to her family	
1643		January-March
	April-July: Writing *Doctrine and Discipline*	

30. Ernest Sirluck, in "Milton's Idle Right Hand," *Milton Studies in Honor of Harris Francis Fletcher* (Urbana: University of Illinois Press, 1961), pp. 141–77, argues that the "failure" of Milton's first marriage (May ? 1642) dealt a paralyzing blow to his poetic inspiration. However, Mary returned sometime around summer 1645. Further, I cannot agree with his concepts of Milton's hopes for poetic achievement, which he dates from at least before December 1629; see "Milton's Decision to Become a Poet," *Modern Language Quarterly* 24 (1963): 21–30. Regardless, the question "Does he return to his poetry?" in April 1642, to which Sirluck responds, "No. Instead, he gets married" (p. 146), can be answered only by finding out what he did do, not by trying to establish the curious equation of poetic achievements and celibacy. Besides, Sirluck has overlooked Milton's words in the Letter to an Unknown Friend (TM, p. 6), dated in the 1630s: "there is besides this, as all well know, about this tyme of a mans life a strong inclination, be it good or no, to build up a house & family of his owne in the best manner he may, . . ." The development of Milton's poetic mind and achievements pursued by Mary Ann Radzinowicz in *Toward Samson Agonistes* (Princeton: Princeton University Press, 1978) likewise should be reviewed.

		August-October
	November-December: Revising *Doctrine and Discipline*	
1644	January: Revising *Doctrine and Discipline*	
		February-April
	May: Writing *Of Education*	
	June-July: Producing *Bucer*	
		August-September
	October-November: Writing *Areopagitica*	
	December: Writing *Tetrachordon* and *Colasterion*	
1645	January-February: Writing *Tetrachordon* and *Colasterion*	
		March-December
	Summer?: Wife returns home	
	Autumn: Readying *Poems* for publication	
1646		January-December
1647		January-December
1648		January-December
1649	January: Writing *Tenure*	
		February-March 15
	March 15-December: Secretary for Foreign Tongues	
	March-October: Writing *Eikonoklastes*	
	May: Writing *Observations upon Articles of Peace*	

Incidental poetry, of course, is not included, and certain undated prose works—*Brief History of Moscovia, Accedence Commenc't Grammar, History of Britain, Long Parliament, Artis Logicæ* —were set down for the most part during the 1640s. We find a total of approximately sixty-six months of "free" time (omitting 1649), or five and a half years within a seven-year period. Despite home activities, it is not, therefore, impossible that much of *Paradise Regain'd* was written during this period.

We have seen that Milton might have proceeded to the temptation as a subject after early 1642 and from the spelling that parts of an early drama may have been composed before around June 1644: "free" time for such preliminary work within these limits seems to total seventeen months. The period from March 1645 to December 1648 (almost four years) allows time for the incomplete development of *Samson Agonistes*, as proposed by William R. Parker, and of *Paradise Regain'd*.

Chapter Three

The Dramatic and Epic Dimensions

FROM the evidence of the Trinity MS notes, it seems that Milton during 1640–42 had hopes of composing various dramas, not one like Elizabethan plays but ones closer to Greek and morality plays. A number of possible subjects from the Bible and from history (both British and Scottish history) are recorded and a few have outline development. They all focus on delimited subjects or events out of what might in someone else's hand have become a broader panorama and a more complex plot. We see this even in a more elaborated scheme like the following:

> Achabæi Cunobaroomeni. 2 Reg. 9. the scene
> Iesrael. beginning frō the watchmans discove-
> ry of Jehu till he go out in the mean
> while message of things passing brought
> to Jesebel &c. lastly the 70 heads of Ahabs
> [so]ns brought in and message brought of
> Ahaziah brethren slain on the way c. 10

The action covers 2 Kings 9:17–20, 30–31 (with 21–29 reported); 10:7–8, 13–14. The use of a nuntius indicates the Greek formulation in Milton's mind and the *epeisodia* would seem to be three, many of the extant Greek dramas having

29

four. In the longer outline for *Baptistes* he talks of a chorus consisting of Lot's shepherds, and his presentation of matter after Jesus has been led away as a result of Judas's betrayal is "by message & chorus" in *Christus patiens*. His "Macbeth" (fortunately unwritten as others have remarked) is described thus: "beginning at the arrivall of Malcolm at Mackduffe, the matter of Duncan may be express't by the appearing of his ghost." The dramatic poem *Samson Agonistes* gives clear proof of the nature of Miltonic drama, whether dated in the forties or the sixties. It also indicates why, in 1670 or thereabouts, he wrote that this example "Of that sort of Dramatic Poem which is call'd Tragedy . . . never was intended . . . to the Stage." He was certainly aware that much drama, including his dramatic poem, did not fit the English stage and his stress is upon poetic genre. He talks, in fact, of "*Æschulus, Sophocles,* and *Euripides*" as "the Three Tragic Poets unequall'd yet by any." Although he was thinking of drama, he was not thinking of *plays* in the theatrical sense.

For *Paradise Regain'd*, comparison with *A Mask*, that is, *Comus*, is instructive as a first attempt at the temptation story. The main "plot" of *A Mask* is the threefold temptation in a wilderness, the central figure in that temptation, the Lady, remaining internally inviolate despite the immanacling of her body. Comus's offer of a glass to assuage her thirst, a version of the first temptation of hunger and necessity, is "put by." "Thou canst not touch the freedom of my mind," she rejoins to Comus's threat to make her an alabaster statue. Comus persists in the temptation by describing "this cordial Julep," which will bring "Refreshment after toil, ease after pain,/That have bin tir'd all day without repast." Again the Lady rejects, saying, "that which is not good is not delicious/To a well-govern'd and wise appetite." Next, Comus argues fraudulently through *concupiscentia oculorum*, offering the riches of the earth, "th' all-worshipt ore and precious gems," which, should the Lady take, would relieve the weight of the "cumber'd" earth and its strangulation by "wast fertility." The pitch to altruistic action has its affinities with the kingdoms temptation, playing upon the selflessness of the one being tempted. But since this also receives no positive response from the Lady, Comus immediately argues rationalizations to try to persuade her to give up her virginity, employing a *carpe rosam* theme and an appeal to vanity. The lure is pride, the *superbia vitæ* of the third temptation, and ultimately an abrogation of her godly being, her chastity (which, of course, is *not* the same as virginity, although many writers on *A Mask* seem to confuse the two). The external being can be controlled, the allegory makes clear, but the internal being can resist the wiles of evil if it is truly "Sun-clad."

From the manuscript of *A Mask* we know that Milton revised frequently—words, lines, passages; that he deleted, replaced, added, and used rejected lines or passages in new positions. To reconstruct either the earliest drafts of the poem or its augmented revision without speculation is impossible on the evidence we have. But the performance-oriented text of September 1634 is not the received reader's text which now exists through its publication in 1637. *Paradise Regain'd* may have undergone similar revisions when first being written (whenever that was) and when readied for publication. The similarity in theme between *Paradise Regain'd* and *A Mask* (a temptation in a wilderness, as we have noted, resisted through the armor of faith) suggests that the earlier masque paved the way to drama on the same theme later on. Now, however, it was to develop the antitype of Jesus and his experience in the wilderness of life; now was to be explored all the tugs upon humankind to forsake moral being and their repulse, in an unambiguously universal lesson.

I have suggested in chapter 2 and have argued previously on the basis of prosodic analysis[1] that *Paradise Regain'd* was begun as a drama in the 1640s, was amplified further a bit later,[2] and was made into epic in the late 1660s. This Greek-influenced dramatic poem would have consisted of longer speeches, little action, and sections standing for a *prologos*, choral odes (*stasima*), *epeisodia*, and an *exodos*. It would not

1. See Shawcross, "The Chronology of Milton's Major Poems."
2. Compare Parker's views in *Milton: A Biography*, vol. 2, pp. 1139–42.

have compounded a number of individual dramas such as Allan H. Gilbert argued lay behind *Paradise Lost*.[3] But it would, I think it is logical to suggest, have equated the Greek dramatic trilogy, of which only Aeschylus' *Oresteia* is an extant model. The threefold temptation is an obvious choice for a trilogy of dramatic poems, each individual drama developing one of the temptations with a capping *exodos* in the third. Like the *Oresteia*, the first two dramas would close at a high emotional pitch, looking forward to the succeeding drama, and the third would present a choral *exodos* of victory. A *kommos*, or final lyric responsive ode between the chorus and a character (in *Eumenides* it is Athena, in *Samson Agonistes* it is Manoa), may have coincided with the *exodos*, as it does in both those dramas. The *exodos* usually included a nuntius' speech and a *deus ex machina*, a main function of whom was to foretell the future.

The first drama in this proposed trilogy would have included a setting of the scene and background, such as Samson's first passage, that is, a *prologos* (the Son's soliloquy, 196–293); a choral ode, or a kind of *parados* (294–320); a long and perhaps composite episode (the first encounter of Satan and Jesus, and its continuance, 321–496); and a kind of brief *exodos* (497–502), ending the current action but implying further action. If indeed Book I of *Paradise Regain'd* was developed out of a drama on the first temptation, such lines in the received text as suggested here as constituting a section of that Greek-influenced drama offer only an approximation of what would have been in the "original." The central temptation and its ensuing discussion between Satan and Jesus breaks into two movements, 321–56 and 357–496, which may have functioned as two episodes for Milton. If the received text was based on such dramatic structure, Milton undoubtedly revised it to make it epical not only by the addition of an epic-related introduction, narrative sections, and speech tags, and by the revision of sections into narrative

3. See Allan H. Gilbert, *On the Composition of Paradise Lost* (Chapel Hill: University of North Carolina Press, 1947; New York: Octagon Books, 1966).

and of prosody, but also perhaps by omission to concentrate the action of the temptation and its immediate aftermath. Further, Milton seems not to have been satisfied with whatever may have been written, for it had remained so long unsung, just as *Paradise Lost*, though its subject had pleased him, long choosing, took a good while to rework and complete. Whatever may have been an earlier writing of *Paradise Regain'd* was clearly not finished; and it was not in such a state that it could have been published without reworking. The dramatic poem was ultimately revised because it was "prompted . . . else mute." (I have noted in chapter 2 Milton's publication in 1669–74 of various earlier items and the posthumous works. One reason why those posthumous works were not published during his lifetime may have been that he did not consider them ready for publication. I think particularly of *A Brief History of Moscovia*.[4] To be noted in this regard, incidentally, is the publication of *Considerations touching the likeliest means to remove Hirelings* in August 1659. The work seems to be an earlier tract—nothing in it dates after 1652, as William B. Hunter has pointed out[5]—with apparently only the dedication and a first paragraph added to introduce the basic tract. Even the last few sentences seem not to be "new." It was published because of Milton's statement of an intended twofold publication in *A Treatise of Civil Power* and the prompting of Moses Wall, who, having read the first, asked after the second.[6])

4. Compare my discussion of this work in my review of volume 8 of the Yale Prose in *Milton Quarterly* 18 (1984): 30–31.

5. See *The Prose of John Milton*, J. Max Patrick, ed., (Garden City: Anchor/Doubleday, 1967), pp. 475–76. Unfortunately, the issue is not raised or pursued in his edition of the work in the Yale Prose. VII, rev. ed. (1980), 229–36.

6. "Two things there be which have bin ever found working much mischief to the church of God, and the advancement of truth; force on the one side restraining [dealt with in *A Treatise of Civil Power*], and hire on the other side corrupting the teachers thereof [dealt with in *Considerations*]. Few ages have bin since the ascension of our Saviour, wherin the one of these two, or both together have not prevaild. It can be at no time therfore unseasonable to speak of these things; since by them the church is either in continual detriment and oppression, or in continual danger. The former shall be at this time my argument; the latter as I shall finde God disposing me, and opportunity inviting" (William B. Hunter, ed., *A Treatise of Civil Power* in the Yale Prose, VII, rev. ed., 241.). It was published in February 1659. Wall's letter, dated 26

The received text of Book I of *Paradise Regain'd* includes the addition of l. 1–7, an introductory passage linking the poem with *Paradise Lost*; 8–17, an invocation to the Spirit as muse; 18–43, a narrative voice setting the context; 106–29, the narrative voice altering the scene from a council in hell to a council in heaven;[7] 168–72, an introduction to the angelic chorus; 173–81, the angelic hymn itself; and 465–67, a brief speech conclusion and introduction.[8] Further additions of Satan's speech to his cohorts (44–105) and of the Father's to the angelic host (130–67) set contrasts between infernal and heavenly intentions and the auditors' antithetical reactions (including 173–81). Section 294–320, which I have cited as that which might have been the *parados*, and section 497–502, which I have cited as that which might have been the *exodos*, exhibit prosody suggesting revision of earlier composition into narrative. Although l. 182–95 prosodically appear to be early, they would logically have been written later to create a transition from the scene in heaven to the desert wild, the *prologos*. One-line speech introductions or speech tags occur in ll. 335, 337, 346, 357, 406, [465–67], 493.

The temptation and the ensuing dialogue, 321–496, even if we think of the passage as two episodes, 321–56 and 357–496, are bare and uncomplicated when looked at alongside a Greek drama. But a work like Aeschylus' *Seven Against Thebes* (the third of a trilogy and including an ending considered spurious) offers some precedent. Almost all the dialogue in Aeschylus' drama is between Eteocles and the Spy (the Messenger) or the Chorus, and only the subject of the fate of Thebes is developed therein. It is circumscribed in subject, characters, and treatment alongside other Greek dramas. The *exodos*, in which Eteocles does not appear, is concerned with

May 1659, remarks, "Sir, my humble Request is, That you wold proceed and give us that other member of the Distribution mentioned in your Book; Sc. that Hire doth greatly impede Truth and Liberty," ibid., p. 512, ed. W. Arthur and Alberta T. Turner. *Considerations*, accordingly, was published in August 1659. The parallel with Ellwood and *Paradise Regain'd* is obvious.

7. A reader will also recognize a residue of the council in hell in Book II of *Paradise Lost* and its contrastive council in heaven in Book III.

8. For detailed prosodic analysis and discussion, see Shawcross, "Chronology."

the fate of the House of Laius. There is a focus, in other words, that has affinities with Milton's concentration of the first temptation. Milton's similar treatment is to alternate speeches between Satan and Jesus: 321–34 (Satan), 335–36 (Jesus), 337–45 (Satan), 347–56 (Jesus), 358–405 (Satan), 407–64 (Jesus), 468–92 (Satan), 494–96 (Jesus). Whatever may have been a chorus has been excised except for what remains as transition between Jesus's soliloquy and the temptation and as the swift close. However, Jesus's sojourn in the wilderness and the interview between Satan and Jesus would logically not be accompanied by other people, and a "chorus" in the Greek dramatic sense with function as a "character" or "characters" would not have existed. Rather, Milton might have handled this as a group framing the action, who stand to the side and observe only. We see this kind of treatment in his use of a chorus in one of his outlines for "Paradise lost" in the Trinity MS. That on p. 35, where he divides his drama into five acts, cites a chorus but does not have that chorus interact with the characters or the action: they are observers, commentators only. In [act 1] a "Chorus of Angels sing a/hymne of ye creation" to complete that act; in act 2 the "chorus sing the marriage song and describe Paradice"; in act 3 the "Chorus feares for Adam and relates Lucifers rebellion and fall"; in act 4 the "Chorus bewails and tells the good Adā hath lost"; in act 5 the "Chorus breifly concludes." There is no hint of the chorus as character or of any verbal interchange with those on the stage.

Book II of *Paradise Regain'd*, as a possible second Greek drama in a trilogy, divides into a chorus of Plain Fishermen (30–57); a prologue by Mary (66–104); a first episode, a further council in hell, with Satan's speech (121–46), followed by Belial's remarks (153–71) and Satan's answer (173–234); a second episode with the Son's soliloquy (245–59), Satan's confrontation and the ensuing dialogue (302–36, 368–401) concerned with the lure of the banquet; and a third episode concerned with the lure of wealth (406–86). Passages of narration, but ones that seem to have undergone later revision into narrative, are ll. 1–29, 105–20, 260–301, and 337–67. If

these four passages were indeed basically earlier speech sec-
tions, they may have been sections of choruses in the first
three instances and part of Satan's speech describing the
banquet in the fourth. Such passages of a chorus might come
from observers of the action rather than a group as a charac-
ter, as suggested before. Brief speech introductions and con-
clusions, added in epic revision, are ll. 58–65, 147–52, 235–
44, 401–5. One-line speech introductions or speech tags occur
in ll. 172, 317, 319, 322, 323, 378, 392, 401, 432. The new
induction, opening chorus, and new soliloquy may therefore
owe their existence in large part to their having been the
beginnings of a second drama on the temptation, this being
given over to the second temptation.

The third book may thus have some relationship with a
second drama devoted to the second temptation, but it seems
also to be a somewhat later expansion of what might have
been the substance of that temptation, spilling over into what
is now Book IV. The third book does not suggest the same
kind of Greek dramatic structural beginning as do books I and
II, but it is almost totally speech passages. Two longer sec-
tions of narrative are included, ll. 251–66 and 310–46; brief
speech introductions or conclusions are ll. 1–6, 145–49,
441–43; and one-line speech introductions or speech tags are
found as or in ll. 43, 108, 121, 181, 150, 203, 386. A develop-
ment in the later 1640s, after the first beginning of what came
to be *Paradise Regain'd*, may have stayed with a dramatic form
but may also have been exploding the boundaries of that
work. A Greek dramatic structure has been transcended. The
identification of the sin of Satan with *regna omnia mundi*, as
Pope observed, and the specificity of much of this book rather
than a more generalized view of the whole temptation motive
backs up this speculation. It also implies dissatisfaction with
the work and with its overall effect, an effect that would have
smacked of disproportion and a lack of unity as drama. *On the
Morning of Christs Nativity* and *Lycidas* are so structurally well
wrought, so balanced in composition and parts, and the
eventual *Paradise Lost* would be as well, that we can under-
stand why Milton would have put aside that current work on

his dramatic trilogy as the responsibilities of 1649 crowded in.

On the other hand, Book IV shows little late writing in the extended narrative passages as well as the speech sections, and its greater comparative length suggests that it may be a composite of a third Greek drama on the third temptation, of that expanded version of the second temptation that Book III argues, and of epic revision. The sections of narrative are ll. 1–43, 394–450, 541–50, 562–95; these may be revisions, according to prosodic statistics, of former choruses or, in the first instance, of an earlier speech passage of Satan. Brief speech introductions or conclusions are ll. 365–67, 484–85, 636–39; one-line speech introductions or speech tags are ll. 109, 154, 170, 195, 285, 499. The angelic hymn of victory, ll. 596–635, furnishes a capping choral *exodos* of victory, while ll. 562–95 represent what might have been the report of a *nuntius* and incorporates the action of the angelic host as a *deus ex machina*. The hymn of victory, however, is specifically revised to reflect comparison with *Paradise Lost*: "Thou . . . hast regain'd lost Paradise" and "A fairer Paradise is founded now/For *Adam* and his chosen Sons."

The received text of *Paradise Regain'd* is dependent upon spoken lines throughout: there are 1,562 full speech lines, or 75.5 percent, and 508 full and partial nonspeech lines, or 24.5 percent. The brief epic as it stands is thus to be viewed in terms of speech act and the dramatic dimension it defines. Milton's kind of drama is not "dramatic" in most people's parlance: *A Mask* and *Samson Agonistes* have had their share of detraction as a result of such "dramatic" lack. But *Paradise Regain'd*, as clearly as these two poems, exhibits the dramatic contest that underlies drama: the Lady and Jesus are pitted against antagonists and meet the challenge from within themselves; Samson is pitted against himself, or rather aspects of himself, exemplified by three people who make attractive the assertion of those challenges. Manoa, Dalila, and Harapha should be viewed less as real personages or antagonists, each *in persona propria*, than as representations of inward forces. In all three cases, nonetheless, the contest defines a dramatic fiction whereby human action, or what could be human action, is imitated by one or more characters. Milton reduces story, or plot, to such an extent that action (and the plotting that would sustain it) is minimal. In *Paradise Regain'd* the action outside the temptation scenes takes place elsewhere as introduction or setting or background, not as something integral to the action of the temptation scenes. The action of the temptation scenes itself is mental and verbal where the protagonist is concerned, rather than physical except for the fraudulent banquet table, the proffered view of the known world and of Rome and Greece, the fraudulent storm, and the ascent to the pinnacle and the denouement (which involves no unraveling of plot or solution to a complication, the more usual ending). The changes and movement within this piece of writing that allow its classification as dramatic are external, as they are in the temptation scenes of *A Mask* and *Samson Agonistes*, except that in the latter Samson undergoes internal development. The Son remains steadfast as does the Lady since there is no reason for change: obedience demands a constant attitude and allows only reaction to that which would alter that attitude and any ensuing action. Samson on the other hand must find steadfastness to the will of Heaven within himself since he has abrogated his relationship through misjudgment, fleshly temptation, and vanity. (Samson is not "regenerated" in the usual sense of that word—a term that has misled criticism of the dramatic poem and caused counter-arguments on both sides: his internal development is the overcoming of *tristitia*, the ascent of patience, and his returned faith in God. There is an internal drama within the dramatic poem.) While the Son does not change and thus while there is no internal drama going on with him (whatever potential change or development there might have been is nullified in the Son's opening soliloquy), it is the external that changes and continues changing while the center holds. Satan must change tactics, even his appearance; he must create illusion, engage in wondrous acts; he alters the seemingly real and empiric to varying degrees of the fanciful and speculative. It is Satan who moves the drama of the poem to an *anagnorisis* and a *peripeteia*.

The Son knows he is the Son of God, despite the unintelligible readings of some critics who have tried to hinge the poem on that question. The Son in his first soliloquy quotes his mother:

> For know, thou art no son of mortal man,
> Though men esteem thee low of Parentage,
> Thy Father is th'Eternal King, who rules
> All Heav'n and Earth, Angels and Sons of men.
>   (I,234–37)

He himself says, "and soon found of whom they spake [Messiah]/I am," and that strongly placed "I am," of course, echoes God's words to Moses; "I AM THAT I AM" (Exod. 3:14). Further, he remarks:

>   my Father's voice,
> Audibly heard from Heav'n, pronounc'd me his,
> Me his beloved Son, in whom *alone* [emphasis mine]
> He was well pleas'd.   (I,283–86)

The *anagnorisis* therefore does not incur the Son's recognition: instead there is Satan's forced acknowledgment of the Son's divinity (after still saying, "if Son of God," l. 555) and the angelic choir's praise of the "True image of the Father . . . Son of the most High." Satan's forced acknowledgment is a dramatic recognition striking the reader as well through the drama of ll. 560–62:[9]

---

9. Compare Arnold Stein's statement of a fourfold *anagnorisis* in *Heroic Knowledge: An Interpretation of Paradise Regained and Samson Agonistes* (Minneapolis: University of Minnesota Press, 1957; rptd., Hamden: Archon Books, 1965), p. 225.

Satan's challenge (ll. 554–59), taken directly from Matthew 4:6 and Luke 4:9–11, makes reference to Psalm 91:11–12, but it suppresses the phrase "to keep thee in all thy ways." As James H. Sims writes, "The promise then, fully quoted, is

> To whom thus Jesus: also it is written,
> Tempt not the Lord thy God, he said and stood.
> But Satan smitten with amazement fell . . .

The biblical phrase "Thou shalt not tempt the Lord thy God" (see Matt. 4:7 and Luke 4:12, which echo Moses's admonition to the Israelites in Deuteronomy 6:16, with its reference to their challenge to God to bring forth water at Massah, Exodus 17:1–7) here allows for the ambiguity that the Lord thy God *the Father* cannot be tempted and that the Lord thy God *the Son* cannot be tempted either, as the full poem has etched so memorably. The dilemma that would have faced an ordinary human, but that does *not* face the Son because of his complete faith, was, of course, to cast himself off the spire and thereby force God the Father to send his ministering angels to save the Son or to stand and surely fall—to death if not the Son of God, safely if the Son of God. But the Son does not face that dilemma and does not, through his being "receiv'd . . . soft/ From his uneasie station," come to recognize his divinity. Like everything else in this dramatic poem, the hero does not undergo the *anagnorisis* found in other dramas experienced by their heroes: it is the antagonist who experiences this effect, just as it has been he who has presented change and has had to manipulate the action. The poem works constantly on reversal of expectation.

The *peripeteia*, occurring with this same final action of the temptation motif, just as *anagnorisis* and *peripeteia* coincide in

---

that the child of God, whether His Son or one of His other children, will be kept from harm *in all his ways*, i.e., in ways that are wise and befitting a child of God. . . . Satan attempts, by the use of Scripture, to tempt Christ to do something which is contrary to the whole spirit of the Scripture verse in its original form" (*The Bible in Milton's Epics* [Gainesville: University of Florida Press, 1962], p. 169). Milton's use of Satan's deceptive challenge is particularly noteworthy when we remember the Son's close knowledge of the Psalms, established earlier in this same poetic book, and when we thus read "thee" in ll. 557 and 558 with recognition that the "thee" does not, in what is written, refer to the Son of God but the auditor—all auditors—of the psalm. Satan (in Matthew and Luke as well as *Paradise Regain'd*) is still wondering about *if* Jesus is the Son of God and is still up to his verbal fraud.

many other dramas, reverses the action or the possibility of any further action and changes, but in a reversal of expectations, on the part of the antagonist, Satan. It resolves the drama with that one line, "But Satan smitten with amazement fell," a line that prosodically keeps the reader at a high pitch and with a sense of continuance until that last word which clangs in one's ears. The reader stops. The reader has a sense of completion and finality and of need to assess the whole that has progressed up to this moment. But the line does not stop: it goes on to a simile encompassing that whole, and then on to another simile, emphasizing Man (the answer to the riddle of the Sphinx) who will be beset by Satan, who has not "died" and who brings his "Joyless triumphals . . . Ruin, and desperation, and dismay" to his cohorts in Hell.[10] The drama has been completed, as the first simile recapitulates, but the substance, we are reminded by the second simile, will continue for all humankind. The Son is now ready to "enter" upon his "glorious work" "and begin to save mankind" (IV.634–35), for mankind has been shown the "pattern of a Christian *Heroe*" and the Son has forged "the rudiments/Of his great warfare"(I.156–57).[11]

The epic text which is *Paradise Regain'd* rests on its narrative and otherwise nonspeech lines, its revision from whatever may have been its dramatic form, and its prosody. The basic definition and elements of an epical work describe Milton's poem: a narrative, with characters of high position, a central figure of heroic proportions, consisting of a series of episodes forming an organic whole, in elevated style, with importance for a nation or race (that is, for humankind). The heroic subject of the temptations encases the foundation of all substantial achievement in the arena of morality and virtue and in conquering the evil which spawns war and man's

10. The reader will remember Satan's announcement of his bad success in Book X of *Paradise Lost*, which is followed by the hissing of the serpents that the fallen angels become and by their partaking of the apples of Sodom.

11. See chapter 5 for further discussion, as well as Robert J. Wickenheiser's "Milton's 'Pattern of A Christian Hero:' The Son in *Paradise Lost*," *Milton Quarterly* 12 (1978): 1–9. The phrase "pattern of a Christian *Heroe*" is from Ralph A. Haug, ed., *The Reason of Church-Government*, in Yale Prose, I.814.

inhumanity to man. The essence of temptation and evil is there, and the means of resistance to or turning back of temptation is there. But these counterstatements to the three temptations come from the Old Testament, as Milton surely knew, from Moses, the prophet "who first taught the chosen Seed." These admonitions and their significance over the years as a way of life illuminate Milton's message and are that message. The epical dimension of Milton's poem lies in the mimesis offered to all people to achieve heroism and advance the race of humankind.

The first temptation in the words of Luke is: "If thou be the Son of God, command this stone that it be made bread. And Jesus answered him, saying, It is written, that man shall not live by bread alone, but by every word of God" (4:3–4). In Deuteronomy 8:3, Moses, recounting the good of the Lord toward the chosen people, says, "And he humbled thee, and suffered thee to hunger, and fed thee with manna, which thou knewst not, neither did thy fathers know; that he might make thee know that man doth not live by bread only, but by every word that proceedeth out of the mouth of the Lord doth man live." The second temptation is: "And the devil, taking him up into a high mountain, showed unto him all the kingdoms of the world in a moment of time. And the devil said unto him, All this power wilt I give thee, and the glory of them: for that is delivered unto me; and to whomsoever I will, I give it. If thou therefore wilt worship me, all shall be thine. And Jesus answered and said unto him, Get thee behind me, Satan: for it is written, Thou shalt worship the Lord thy God, and him only shalt thou serve" (4:5–8). Moses, warning the Israelites against disobedience after the Lord had brought them to a new land, inveighs: "Thou shalt fear the Lord thy God, and serve him, and shalt swear by his name. Ye shall not go after other gods, of the gods of the people which are round about you" (Deut. 6:13–14). Particularly appropriate to the second temptation and Milton's expansion to include wealth are Moses's further words: "And thou say in thine heart, My power and the might of mine hand hath gotten me this wealth. But thou shalt remember the Lord thy God: for it is he that giveth the power to get wealth, that he may establish his covenant which he sware unto thy fathers, as it is this day. And it shall be, if thou do at all forget the Lord thy God, and walk after other Gods, and serve them, and worship them, I testify against you this day that ye shall surely perish. As the nations which the Lord destroyeth before your face, so shall ye perish; because ye could not be obedient unto the voice of the Lord your God" (Deut. 8:17–20). Jesus employs the rejection "Get thee behind me" in *Paradise Regain'd* IV.193, just after the completion of the kingdoms temptation. The third temptation in Luke (the second in Matthew) is given thus: "And he brought him to Jerusalem, and set him on a pinnacle of the temple, and said unto him, If thou be the Son of God, cast thyself down from hence. . . . And Jesus answering said unto him, It is said, Thou shalt not tempt the Lord thy God" (4:9, 12). In remembrance of an event to which I have already alluded, Moses reminds his people, "Ye shall not tempt the Lord your God, as ye tempted him in Massah" (Deut. 6:16). Indeed, the whole of the Son's temptation in the wilderness of forty days (the length of Noah's trial, Moses' retreat to the mount, and also Elijah's) is paralleled by the experience of the Israelites: "And thou shalt remember all the way which the Lord thy God led thee these forty years in the wilderness, to humble thee, and to prove thee, to know what was in thine heart, whether thou wouldst keep his commandments, or no" (Deut. 8:2). The word *prove* here means both *test* and *establish the worth of.*[12]

These epical matters concerning the Israelites, the chosen seed, as well as all of God's children, are the timeless and universal concerns of humankind. From the proem to Book

---

12. There is a tradition that Adam spent forty days in the garden of Eden before the creation of Eve, probably developed by exegetes later on because forty came to symbolize privation and trial and because they wished to equate the first Adam's experience with the biblical account of the second Adam's. Thus the Son's temptation by Satan and its defeat, rather than the Crucifixion, became the reversal of Adam's failure of obedience. Such spurious paralleling, of course, rests on a false equation of the "proving" of the Son and Adam's lack of trial at that time; but it does give insight into the thinking of the church fathers. See also J. M. Evans, *"Paradise Lost" and the Genesis Tradition* (Oxford: Clarendon Press, 1968), p. 104.

IX of *Paradise Lost*, at least, we know that for Milton such warfare against the arms of Satan, Sin, and Death, is "more Heroic then the wrauth/Of stern *Achilles*." And we know that "the better fortitude/Of Patience and Heroic Martyrdom" "justly gives Heroic name/To Person or to Poem." *Paradise Regain'd*, celebrating Patience and preparing for a Martyrdom to come, calmly but unrelentingly attempts "to repair the ruins of our first parents" directly, unambiguously, preceptively. This may be accomplished "by regaining to know God aright, and out of that knowledge to love him, to imitate him, to be like him, as we may the neerest by possessing our souls of true vertue, which being united to the heavenly grace of faith makes up the highest perfection."[13] (The biblical references are to 1 John 3:2 and 2 Peter 1:5–8.) This passage from Milton's 1644 *Of Education* has often been linked with *Paradise Lost*, but it is more striking as an analogue to and critique of *Paradise Regain'd*. The figure of the Son who so marvelously demonstrates "the heavenly grace of faith" and "the highest perfection" is the hero shown to be like God, although he is the man Jesus, totally emptied of godhead. This "justly gives Heroic name/To Person [and] to Poem." The mimesis implied in the quotation from the prose tract is the mimesis of the drama presented in *Paradise Regain'd*. And the thinking that that prose tract records in 1644 adds further credence to the earlier beginning of what came to be Milton's brief epic, what he had to say about "Paradise found."

13. Donald C. Dorian, ed., *Of Education* in Yale Prose, II.366–67.

Chapter Four

Structure

THE basic structure of *Paradise Regain'd* is that of the triple equation of the flesh, the world, and the devil.[1] This can be described in various ways: *concupiscentia carnis, concupiscentia oculorum,* and *superbia vitæ*; or hunger, kingdoms, and the tower; or necessity, fraud, and violence; or the role of the Son as prophet, as king, and as priest. The first temptation investigates man's relationship with the self; the second, with community; the third, with his God. The sin that is tempted in the first is gluttony, and the doctrinal answer is that man lives not by bread alone, but by every word of God. The sin that is tempted in the second is avarice, and the answer is, "Get thee behind me, Satan," for a good man shall worship God and serve Him only. The sin that is tempted in the third is pride, and the answer is, "Thou shalt not tempt the Lord thy God." Milton has placed the first temptation in Book I; the second temptation is spread through books II, III, and IV; and the third temptation is in Book IV. Pertinently, Ely Starr in *Les*

---

1. See Pope, *Paradise Regained,* and Lewalski, *Milton's Brief Epic.* Although the relationship of the tradition of the triple equation to Milton's poem should be reconsidered in certain ways, for parts of Pope's discussion are not pertinent, my ensuing discussion is derived in large part from both these books. Refer also to diagram 1.

The fullest demonstration of the triadic structure is that by Patrick Cullen in *Infernal Triad: The Flesh, the World, and the Devil in Spenser and Milton* (Princeton: Princeton University Press, 1974), ch. 4: "The Structure of *Paradise Regained,*" pp. 125–81.

Mystères de l'Être (Paris, 1902) saw ternary structure—that is, any arrangement involving three items—in terms of intuition (or moral light), thought (or intellectual light), and instinct (or animal light), and these are the stresses of the three temptations. The Son rejects the stones-into-bread motif by an intuition: "I discern thee other then thou seem'st," he says in I.348, and asks, "Why dost thou then suggest to me distrust,/Knowing who I am, as I know who thou art?" (I.355–56). He rejects all the facets of the second temptation through thought; for example, in response to Satan's charge that God exacts pronounced glory from his foes, the Son replies, "And reason" (II.122). The faith that resolves the dilemma of the third temptation—to cast himself off the tower and thereby challenge God to prove himself or to remain standing and soon fall to otherwise certain death—is immediate, not considered, instinctual. Not all commentators on the poem have seen it as I describe it, and unfortunately once a view gets into print we seem to be stuck with it though a number of prior statements have been shown to be insubstantial.[2]

The first temptation teaches abstemiousness, but its main concern is that man know himself well, his capabilities, his stamina, and his control of body by mind. It calls forth the cardinal virtue of temperance. Without such knowledge of Self man becomes prey to all other temptations and cannot develop within himself the other virtues of prudence, justice, or fortitude.

The second temptation is divided into three general divisions, each however tempting avarice, each built on fraud, and each dealing with one's relationship to community. The second temptation deals with material things, since the community so often rates man by his material possessions and therefore by his community position. James McAdams has revived former misinterpretations concerning Satan's banquet

2. For a review of most of this differing opinion, see Burton J. Weber, "The Schematic Structure of *Paradise Regained*: A Hypothesis," *Philological Quarterly* 50 (1971): 553–66.

and the storm, in regard to the three temptations.[3] He erroneously casts the "Night of Dream" and the banquet in Book II as temptations of the flesh (that is, to gluttony) and Athens and the "night of Storm" in Book IV as temptations of the devil (that is, to vainglory). He thus places the "Night of Storm" within the second temptation and argues that the second temptation consists of the three temptations of the flesh, the world, and the devil. While there are linkages between the first stages of the second temptation with the first temptation and the third stages of the second temptation with the third temptation, these are *all* part of the second temptation and they *all* invoke avarice only. They involve man's relationship with community and unnecessary abundance as a sign of community esteem. The Son does not reject food in the banquet scene but delicious cates, nor does he deny basic knowledge but conjectural doctrines and oratory. It is the unnecessary and pluralistic that is rejected. This cannot be stressed too strongly, for many critics have missed the point as reference to Weber's article will indicate. What seem to be overlooked are, first, Jesus's answer to Satan's examples of those whose hunger has been alleviated by providing angels: "They all had need, I as thou seest have none" (II.318); and, second, the Son's own ability to "command a Table in this Wilderness" (II.384) had he such need, and his contemning of the "pompous Delicacies" (II.390) offered by Satan. The Son has said that he will eat "as I like/The giver" (II.321–22), and he rightly counts Satan's "specious gifts no gifts but guiles" (II.391). The temptation is fraudulent, not of necessity, and it is materialistic, not concerned with man's essential life needs.

The first division of the second temptation is divided into two. The lure *voluptaria* takes two related forms: sexual appetite and the ingestion of food. Belial proposes that the fallen angels set women in the Son's eye and in his walk, which idea Satan rejects. Instead, shortly afterward, Satan produces a

3. James R. McAdams, "The Pattern of Temptations in *Paradise Regained*," *Milton Studies* 4 (1972): 177–93.

sumptuous table of foods, which the Son rejects. In both cases
the potential sin of avarice is in play, for man has the *necessity*
of sexual release and of nourishment, but he does not need
numerous sexual partners or the treasured cates offered with
harpy wings. Belial's women are obviously not to be what they
appear, and Satan's feast is presented as being in accord with
Hebraic law, though it is not. In neither case is necessary
alleviation of appetite involved; both are excessive, and both
are fraudulent. The community view of the man who has, as it
were, more than his basic share or need—whether amorous
conquests or expensive and rich foods—is often, regrettably,
high. This second temptation in the wilderness of life to which
man so frequently succumbs teaches that accumulation be-
yond necessity is the work of the devil and that no man so
endowed can any longer serve only God, but rather he serves
those material things and the political-economic ethic which
must be devised to maintain them.[4] The lure of *voluptaria* is
presented in Book II, but it is evident that it looks backward
to the first temptation. It is a perfect example of fraud because
it only *appears* to be related to the first temptation—and some
early commentators and others have been taken in by that
appearance—but whereas the first dealt with what the Self
considers its essential needs and what actually are, this temp-
tation deals entirely with the excessive beyond necessity. Its
placement allows the reader to make a telling comparison
between necessity and excess. We may note as well that
Milton avoids a delicate problem by having sexual appetite,
for some and popularly the most unresisting of all tempta-
tions, brought into consideration for the Son of God by
indirect means.

The second division of the second temptation is the lure
activa, and this takes three forms: wealth, presented at the end
of Book II and linking the lure of *voluptaria* with what follows;

4. For the whole concept developed in the second temptation, we should compare
the Lady's remarks in *Comus*, "If every just man that now pines with want/Had but a
moderate and beseeming share/Of that which lewdly-pamper'd Luxury/Now heaps
upon some few with vast excess,/Natures full blessings would be well dispens't . . ."
(768–72). The Son's saying he will eat "as I like/The giver" is not different from the
Lady's "none/But such as are good men can give good things" (702–3).

glory, presented in Book III; and kingdom, presented in books III and IV. The second division again presents material possessions or position through fraud. First, Satan argues that "Money brings Honour, Friends, Conquest, and Realms" (and unfortunately he is right), but his examples are Antipater and Herod. Next, Satan denigrates God as one who seeks glory, but he equates such glory with tyranny and subservience. And third, Satan offers to make the Son king of all the known world at once, but advises joining Parthia against Rome, among other things. Each is fraudulent, but the Son is not, and should not be, concerned with exposing the fraud; he is concerned with rejecting any appeal that avarice may have for him as man, that is, for man, since avarice is built on self-hate and what we today label the antiheroic. When man thinks so little of himself that he must aggrandize himself in the eyes of his community through accumulation of material things and power (and in the next division of this second temptation it will be by intellectual power), he has partaken of the antiheroic since he does not accept himself and others as he and they are. The message of the last two elements of this section of the triple equation is that man should accept life as it is rather than shaking some vain fist at the sun and trying to raise himself from his self-conceived insect state. This does not counsel passivity, however, nor resignation, but rather to start with what is and actively use that.

McAdams's manipulation of the poem to fit a symmetric scheme (see diagram 2) casts the first section of the second temptation as part of the transitional scene; places the first part of the specific kingdoms temptation, Israel, as the focal section; excludes from that temptation ll. 195–211. in Book IV, which certainly are part of that temptation, ending significantly, "therefore let pass, as they are transitory,/The Kingdoms of this world; I shall no more/Advise thee, gain them as thou canst, or not"; and makes the storm scene part of the full second temptation. The scheme of organization is devised to stress symmetry and thus to emphasize the centrality of the Israel section, which McAdams says, "is thematically as well as structurally central in the scheme of temptation," the

"thematic crux, or perhaps microcosm, of the poem." It
should be evident that the poem is not symmetric, and that
the seeming symmetry of the treatment of temptation two in
books II–IV (see diagram 1) is not really symmetric. Book
III picks up a different division of 2B whereas Book IV
continues the division of 2B begun in Book III. What we have
is balance if we give all parts equal weight, although some
parts (2Bc1, 2Bc2, 2Bc3) are components of a larger part
(2B), which is a component of a still larger part (temptation
2). The Israel section, 2Bc1 (III.149–243), is, surely, impor-
tant, but anyone who can see this section as a microcosm of
the poem is not reading the poem written by Milton. In a
different approach, Weber omits the Belial section and builds
a structure based on a triple triad of sense, reason, and
intellect (see diagram 3). The subdivided appeals of the
second temptation do involve sense, reason, and intellect, and
Milton may consciously have stressed one or the other in the
various sections as outlined by Weber. His scheme is, we
might note, not symmetric. But his symmetric scheme of
biblical and extrabiblical events (see diagram 4) oversim-
plifies and somewhat wrests the perspective. All it says, I
think, is that the three elements of the basic temptation motif
in Matthew and Luke are surrounded by episodes not specifi-
cally cited in the Bible.

The third division of the second temptation presents the
lure of *contemplativa* in Book IV and uses the metaphor of
unnecessary knowledge, presented as philosophy or in writing
or oratory (poetry), for the only *necessary* knowledge for man is
God's word. The philosophy and poetry of the Psalms are
sufficient for any man; all else is interpretation of God's word,
though necessary for those who cannot interpret for them-
selves. Satan's fraud is to argue that such philosophy and
poetry will render the Son a king complete within himself. It
harkens toward the third temptation since it suggests that
such knowledge will make one a rival of God. It is comparable
to the course that Faustus takes. What the total second
temptation teaches is charity toward all men as equals, an
equality of wealth and glory and position for all men, and that
to serve man, rather than to tyrannize him by materialism or

Diagram 1: General Scheme

Book	Lines	Temp-tation	Form	Method	Role	Vice	Virtue	Relationship
I	314–502	1	*concupiscentia carnis* flesh hunger	necessity	prophet	gluttony	temperance	with Self
II		2	*concupiscentia oculorum* world kingdoms	fraud	king	avarice	prudence	with community
			A *voluptaria*					
	153–234		a. sexual appetite					
	298–405		b. bodily appetite					
			B *activa*					
	406–86		a. wealth					
III	108–44		b. glory					
	150–		c. kingdom					
IV	–211							
			C *contemplativa*					
	212–		a. philosophy					
	–364		b. poetry					
	397–580	3	*superbia vite* devil tower	violence	priest	pride (vainglory)	fortitude	with God

Diagram 2:
Reference Scheme for Discussion of McAdams's Article

I	II	III	IV		II	III	IV
1	2A				2A		
	2Ba	2Bb			2Ba	2Bb	
		2Bc	2Bc	OR		2Bc1	
			2C			2Bc2	2Bc3
			3				2C
							3

Diagram 3: Weber's Scheme

1	2A: SENSE			
	2B: REASON			
	2Ba: Sense	2Bb: Intellect		
		2Bc: Reason		
		2Bc1: intellect		
		2Bc2: sense	2Bc3: reason	
			2C: INTELLECT	
			3	

Diagram 4:
Paradise Regain'd
Biblical and Extrabiblical Materials

Day of Temptation

1	beginning: biblical
	ending: extrabiblical
2	beginning: extrabiblical
	middle: biblical
	ending: extrabiblical
3	beginning: extrabiblical
	ending: biblical

power or high-flown oratory and intellectual elitism, is to
serve God. It evokes the cardinal virtues of prudence and
justice.

Thus in development from the preceding, the third tempta-
tion involves the virtue of fortitude as well as faith. This
component of the triple equation has been introduced by a
storm that the Son endures through these two virtues, al-
though exercise of his will is not called up as it will be in the
tower temptation, and the storm links the second and third
temptations since it is not a real storm, that is, one from
natural causes, but rather has been conjured up by the
fraudulent Satan. There is no corresponding linkage between
the first and second temptations, and I believe this is so on
purpose. McAdams parallels the Son's dream of eating
(II.245–84) with the storm scene. Such a scheme forces
Belial's argument out of the temptation motif entirely, dis-
uniting it from the banquet scene, and misses an important
subtlety. The dream is not a transition into a new temptation
but part of a broader section. The interrelationships between
sex and eating can be evidenced by natural observation and
thus their mutuality is recognized by myth and religion, not
only by Freud. The dream sequence develops a hint in Satan's
answer to Belial (appropriately in a context of sleep) and
prepares for the banquet scene which follows. Note it is
"appetite" that "is wont to dream." The form of Satan's
temptation is adumbrated and divine counsel is given to the
Son. A dream frequently has the function of achieving tran-
scendence, by which I mean a transformation of personality
through the blending and fusion of noble with base compo-
nents or of the conscious with the unconscious. The poten-
tially base components of the Son's dream are nullified by the
example of Elijah, just as Man's base components can in the
future be transcended by the example of the Son. The only
similar function that the storm has is foreshadowing the next
temptation, but not in form, in method, not through advice
sent through example, but through an attempt to intimidate.
The Son remains unshaken, and does not, apparently, even
consider whether these seemingly natural occurrences come

from God's showing his displeasure or not, for he has learned
previously to be patient with his lot. Contrast lies in the
"truth" of the dream and the fraudulence of the storm, in the
naturalness of the Son's sleep and its surroundings and the
unnaturalness of the storm and its surroundings. The storm
yields a foreview of potential though quite different violence to
come; rather than give divine counsel, it tries to disturb the
sleep with ugly dreams. But dreams do not constitute tempta-
tion as McAdams would have it, even in modern psychology;
they may show only the effects of temptation or the anxieties
over being tempted. And Satan says:

> Since neither wealth, nor honour, arms nor arts,
> Kingdom nor Empire pleases thee, nor aught
> By me propos'd in life contemplative,
> Or active, tended on by glory, or fame,
> What dost thou in this World?   (IV.368ff.)

which certainly separates what is to follow in the wilderness
(that is, the storm) from what has preceded. The storm is
transitional between temptation two and temptation three;
there is metaphoric contrast with the earlier dream at best.

The storm makes smoothly continuous the narrative of
Book IV as the poem moves forward. Such a corresponding
linkage earlier would nullify or replace the full break between
books I and II and the new induction and beginning in Book
II. In other words, this major break between the first two
books of the poem with a new invocation and start in Book II,
not adequately examined previously, points to a very definite
decision on Milton's part. This decision must have had a
purposeful aim. What thus appears within the poem is a
structure of one book against three books as a linked unit.
While there are four books, and this is significant, we also
have a ratio of one to three. The treatment of the first and
second books throws the first book into relief against the other
three, and the last three books become a unit unto themselves.

The significance of this structure is mythic, and its reason for being will be taken up in the following chapter. But first another curiosity should be looked at.

The four books of *Paradise Regain'd* are, unto themselves, disproportionate in length: Book I has 502 lines; Book II, 486 lines; Book III, 443 lines; and Book IV, 639 lines. Book I, 502 lines, thus contrasts with books II–IV, 1,568 lines, being just less than a fourth of the total poem (24.2 percent). The ideal of the golden mean (in art, the golden section) proposed that the focal point of interest lay roughly in a .618 to .382 ratio between some greater and some lesser division.[5] The golden mean emphasizes the fact that symmetry is *not* traditionally considered the most artistic of structural principles and that interest lies in balancings and weights. In Book I the first temptation begins at l. 314, "But now an aged man in Rural weeds." Its position is .625 into the book, and thus the induction, the scene in Hell, the scene in Heaven, and the Son's soliloquy in the wilderness of Earth are all balanced by the temptation scene of only 189 lines. The victory of the Self in the first temptation counters the hoped-for success of Satan, illustrates God's words that "From what consummate vertue I have chose/This perfect Man, by merit call'd my Son" (165–66), and resolves the Son's question of "What from within I feel my self, and hear/What from without comes often to my ears" (198–99). The weight given the first temptation is paradoxically enhanced by its briefer length.

In Book II the focus occurs after the induction and Mary's soliloquy, the scene in Hell, and the Son's dream, "When suddenly a man before him stood,/Not rustic as before, but seemlier clad" (298–99). This is again the beginning of Satan's direct confrontation of the Son, and it is .613–.615 into the second book. Balancing the beginnings of Book II are the lures of the fraudulent banquet and of wealth. The Son's rejection of the banquet and of wealth is consonant with the

5. The figures are derived from the series 1, 2, 3, 5, 8, 13, 21, 34, 55, 89, 144, 233, 377, 610, 987, 1597, and so on, where the third term of a triad is the sum of the first two terms of that triad. The first term is in a ratio of .382 to the sum; the second term, in a ratio of .618. That is, for example: 1597 divided into 987 is .618.

kind of persons Andrew and Simon Peter are: Plain Fisher-
men, who reside "in a Cottage low." For them Jesus is "our
hope, our joy" (5). His rejection corroborates, metaphorically,
Mary's faith that he could not lose himself. While Satan can
accuse Belial of judging others by himself, we see that Satan's
"manlier objects," which in this book "only seem to
satisfie/Lawful desires of Nature, not beyond," reflect his, not
the Son's, goods.

In Book III after a dialogue moving from the lure and
rejection of wealth of the prior book to the lure and rejection of
glory (108–44), and after the first lure of kingdom, that of
Israel (149–243), Satan removes the Son to a mountain below
which can be viewed the kingdoms of the known Eastern
world. This central section of the kingdoms temptation, lying
after the symbolic kingdom of Israel and before the ephemeral
and specific Western kingdom of the city of Rome in Book IV,
begins with l. 267, which is .602 into Book III. As focus it
throws up a contrast between the more abstract discussions of
glory and symbolic kingdom and the very palpable lands to be
ruled by Parthia or Rome. Such a contrast demands that the
lure of a specific government, Rome, be placed in another
book in order to separate it sufficiently to allow the contrast
between abstract and actual kingdom to remain sharp. (Com-
pare Satan's "A Kingdom they portend thee, but what
Kingdom,/Real or Allegoric I discern not" [IV.389–90].) For
Book III the focus around l. 267 moves us from the personal
and discursive lures of glory and Israel's kingdom to relation-
ship and specificity. Up to this point in the poem all the lures
have turned on a personal pitch: hunger, sexual appetite,
bodily appetite, wealth, glory, and even Israel (of which the
Son says, "Know'st thou not that my rising is thy fall,/And
my promotion will be thy destruction?" [201–2]). After this
point the lures involve relationship: first, Parthia's or Rome's
relationship with the lands to be ruled; then, in Book IV,
Rome's relationship with "All Nations [which] not to *Rome*
obedience pay"; next, control of man's mind through philoso-
phy and oratory; and finally, a direct confrontation with God
himself. This kingdoms section, 2Bc2, is the focal motif of the

poem (once one forgets about symmetry) (see diagram 1):1, 2Aa, 2Ab, 2Ba, 2Bb, 2Bc1, *2Bc2*, 2Bc3, 2Ca 2Cb, 3. It is the seventh section of eleven. The position of the golden mean of the entire poem is III.291, which falls within this section. It becomes a watershed for the poem, separating Satan's appeals to what are more personal lures from his appeals to a superiority over others, including God, through forcing his decree to be put to a test.

In Book IV, after the second temptation has been completed, the storm scene presents a transition into the third temptation. The storm scene, beginning at l. 394, becomes the focal point of this book: it is .616 into the book. The storm yields a foreview of potential though quite different violence to come, as stated earlier. As the narrative voice says, "ill wast thou shrouded then,/0 patient Son of God, yet only stoodst/ Unshaken" (419–21),[6] and this is to be the Son's resolution in the tower temptation: "he said and stood./But Satan smitten with amazement fell" (561–62). The focal point does not occur with Satan's entry into this book *in propria persona* (451) because he is not disguised as in books I and II and he explicitly calls Jesus the Son of God, though he still wishes to know how divine this Man/God is. What is to follow is the venting of his rage, not some "new device," for "they all were spent." Satan, of course, has not learned—he still proclaims that "each act is rightliest done,/Not when it must, but when it may be best" (475–76)—but he is not now trying to deceive the Son by fraud. Rather he tries to argue from what has been written to challenge its truth and raise doubts through contrary possibilities until what has been written is put to the test. Thus the focal position of the storm emphasizes the potential violence of the third temptation, throwing into relief the change in Satan's tactics and attitude which the remainder of the book depicts.

The sections in each book of *Paradise Regain'd* created by

6. That word "shrouded" sets up in the attentive reader's mind the contrast with a "good" shrouding, after the Crucifixion, toward which, for the Christian, the history of the Son following upon the close of the poem will lead. The greatest concept of good possible will then have arisen out of the greatest concept of evil.

attention to the golden mean yield meaning for the full work
and the artistic construct. That such attention was paid by
Milton will be patent to some readers and I assume farfetched
to others. But authors did—and do—write with such attention
being paid, and the demonstrable significance of the golden
mean to *Paradise Regain'd* cannot, I believe, be discarded as
coincidence. The lengths of the books seem thus to be a
function of this attention with, to recapitulate, the following
importances: Book I is roughly a quarter of the whole, al-
though no other book is; the focus of the golden mean may
point to the beginning of direct temptation; the focus of the
golden mean may contrast what has preceded with what will
follow; the focus of the golden mean may delineate a new stage
in the approach to temptation; and the treatment of Book III
in terms of the focus of the golden mean demands the exclu-
sion of the third part of the kingdoms temptation from that
book, thus partially accounting for the somewhat dispropor-
tion of Book IV.

Chapter Five

Mythic Substruct

I have already remarked on the basic reason for the curious separation of Book I from the rest of *Paradise Regain'd*: human beings must come to such knowledge of Self that no temptation will have effect upon them. Only through prior knowledge of the Self can one develop later prudence, or justice toward one's fellow humans, or fortitude. The separated and unitive impression that we receive from Milton's treatment of his text emphasizes the individual being. While the temptation motif encased in the Gospels presents an epitome of all the temptations that humanity may undergo in life, and while it epitomizes as well the means to resist such temptation in order, like the Son himself, to become worthy in God's eyes, Milton's treatment of this "plot" adds emphases and analyses of interrelationships of its parts. The first emphasis we observe—and which seems not to have been observed in the past—is the precedence of the first temptation. Once it is truly conquered, the remaining motifs of temptation will not have a chance of being effective. The separation of Book I from the rest of the poem and the unifying of the rest of the poem into one extensive unit underscore this point and make it unavoidable, even though commentators who have not really been concerned with Milton's literary achievement have overlooked it.

Book I is given over to the resolution of the multitude of thoughts that swarm within the Son as he considers what from within he feels and what from without he hears. And the remainder of the poem is *not* concerned with the Son's determination of his being the Father's Son or of his role.[1] It is concerned with the form that the role will take. It is unfortunate that modern commentators have tried to force Milton to have written some kind of suspense story, in which the drama is supposed to revolve around the protagonist's uncertainty of identity and life purpose. Such commentators, it seems to me, have a narrow view of what literature is and of how to appreciate it.

The emphasis on the Self in Book I is enhanced by the conception of oneness evoked in placement of the temptation entirely and only in Book I and by the sharp break. The number one implies godhead and the divine; Milton's treatment of this temptation of flesh (the clearest example of the nature of humankind) demands that we see the unity of the nature of man and the godlike nature (or soul) within the one man Jesus. That is, he is true man; but true man, being created in God's image, may exhibit godlike virtue. The trial of the wilderness will expose the rudiments of Jesus's great warfare: humiliation (or faith) and strong sufferance (or obedience), so that he will be able to enter on his glorious

---

1. Arthur Barker summarizes the frequent modern view thus: "We have come to recognize that the main burden of the poem is the progressive discovery by the Christ, who is at that point passing from youth to maturity, of the meaning of that declaration for him. He is, our critics have made clear, discovering the character of his mediatorial office and what it implies for himself and for men" ("Calm Regained through Passion Spent: The Conclusion of the Miltonic Effort," in *The Prison and the Pinnacle*, ed. Balachandra Rajan [Toronto: University of Toronto Press, 1973], pp. 21–22). It will be clear that I agree, instead, with Irene Samuel's position in a fine article in the same collection, "The Regaining of Paradise," pp. 111–34. Rejecting identity crisis as the central concern of the brief epic, Samuel discusses the way in which Milton answers the question, "How is man to live?"; that is, the poem, concerned with the choice of a life-style, presents "the mimesis of a universal action, a program for every man" (p. 126). The important lines 560–61 of Book IV:

Tempt not the Lord thy God, he said and stood.
But Satan smitten with amazement, fell

I also read as reference to not putting God to a test of miraculous power (as in Deut. 6:16); I see them as saying nothing about identity, but unlike others I believe that the Son has no question of his identity after Book I.

work and begin to save humankind after he returns to his
mother's house. The treatment of the Son in the poem shows
how Man can develop within himself the "Paradise within,
happier farr," the postlapsarian Paradise open to all men, as
Gary D. Hamilton has argued.[2]

The Son has come to acknowledge his mission from God by
the end of Book I:

> God hath now sent his living Oracle
> Into the World, to teach his final will.   (I.460–61)

He recognizes that he is that manifestation:

> [God] sends his spirit of Truth henceforth to dwell
> In pious Hearts, an inward Oracle
> To all Truth requisite for men to know   (I.462–64)

(Note here the relationship with the *contemplativa* section of the
second temptation.) The emphasis in Book I clearly is upon
the inward being of this man. The Son's understanding of that
Self and its limitations rejects both self-aggrandized power (to
be tested in the second temptation) and pride (to be tested in
the third temptation) when he declines to bid or forbid Satan
to do anything:

> do as thou find'st
> Permission from above; thou canst not more.   (I.495–96)

Although Book I is not linked to Book II, which begins,
"Mean while the new-baptiz'd, who yet remain'd/At *Jordan*

2. Gary D. Hamilton, "Creating the Garden Anew: The Dynamics of *Paradise Regained*," *Philological Quarterly* 50 (1971): 567–84.

with the Baptist," its final lines anticipate the temptations
that will be proffered the Son and the basic attitude which will
reject them. In these final lines we also have a foretaste of
Satan's ploys. He talks of his parting from truth "If it may
stand him more in stead to lie,/Say and unsay, feign, flatter,
or abjure." And accordingly he dissembles by flattery when he
says he delights to hear the dictates of Truth from the Son's
mouth, adding that the Son would suffer him just as the
Father suffers the hypocrite and the atheous priest. But the
Son remains aloof, knowing like a younger Milton that he will
be led by time and the will of heaven since all is in the great
taskmaster's eye.

The context of Book I is mythic. As in mythic rituals of
initiation, Jesus's identity is dissolved through his opening
soliloquy into the collective unconscious represented by the
wilderness of the world in which he finds himself, once sepa-
rated from his mother's house. In his soliloquy he recounts his
life up to that point; what is to come is obviously a new phase.
Through the temptations of Satan in this book—as aged man
in rural weeds, first, and then as Archfiend undisguised—the
Son is reborn into the new phase to come. He has rejected the
false advice of the elder, of the supposedly experienced; but at
the same time he has rejected the undermining of faith in the
past. Jesus, like man entering upon the adult world, must
separate truth from lies, things of real worth from false values,
action by precept from action by fear, and pleasures of good
and lastingness from pleasures of doing ill and the ephemeral.
He must recognize Satan as trickster, for Satan in Book I is
the shaman of initiation ritual whose world involved magic.
The Son must reject the magical and accept the factual. For
Erik H. Eriksen in *Childhood and Society* the fifth stage in man's
development is puberty and adolescence, which are charac-
terized by identity versus role confusion. What Book I of
Paradise Regain'd achieves is identity for the Son so that the
roles hinted at but undetermined in the soliloquy are finally
understood. The soliloquy suggests that Jesus has moved
through the prior stages or oral-sensory (developing basic
trust), muscular-anal (accepting autonomy), locomotor-

genital (moving to initiative), and latency (exhibiting indus-
try). And of course these are observable in the life of the Son
up to this point, particularly when we remember his entry into
the Temple and his confounding of the doctors. Once the
identity of the Son as man is established, he is able to pursue
his adult world as represented by the temptations of books II,
III, and IV. That identity is achieved by breaking any re-
maining mother-child identity and taking on the energy of the
Father. The return to his Mother's house at the end of the
brief epic indicates on one level the fullness of his life as
individual man at that point and a metaphoric return to the
womb (a death symbol), and on another level it represents the
achievement of a form for the energy (or power) that has been
developed through the temptations. Energy, an attribute of
the father, implies action and wisdom; form, an attribute of
the mother, implies tangible structures or patterns through
which energy will work. The glorious work on which the Son
will now enter to save mankind will combine the energy which
the temptations have developed and the pattern of meekness
which transcends from the mother.

One way of looking at books II–IV of *Paradise Regain'd* is to
see this section as representative of the form that the energy
developed in Book I takes: significantly, "meek" or "meekly"
is used only three other times in the poem besides that in the
last four lines. It is used of Mary in II.108; of the Son in the
midst of the kingdoms temptation in III.217, by Satan who
wishes the Son to intercede for him with the Father; and again
of the Son in IV.401, just before the storm. The concept of
meekness thus opens (after the induction) and closes the unit
of the poem constituted by books II, III, and IV; is specifi-
cally associated with the mother and return to the mother's
house; is used with fraudulent purpose by Satan but with
knowledge that the Son's "placid aspect and meek regard"
can intercede with the Father's Truth; and is assigned to one
who has already shown submissiveness and patience in the
second temptation. (Satan's use of the word appears in a
sexually fraught passage, we should note: "A shelter and a
kind of shading cool/Interposition, as a summers cloud.")

Psalm 25:9–10 reads: "The meek will he guide in judgment:
and the meek will he teach his way. All the paths of the Lord
are mercy and truth unto such as keep his covenant and his
testimonies," the point really of the tower temptation, and
Matthew 11:28–30 quotes Jesus as the Son and the only one
through whom the Father can be revealed: "Come unto me,
all ye that labor and are heavy laden, and I will give you rest.
Take my yoke upon you, and learn of me; for I am meek and
lowly in heart: and ye shall find rest unto your souls. For my
yoke is easy, and my burden is light." The hints of female
imagery and woman's traditional submissiveness to the male
should be rather obvious. We might also compare *Elegia
quinta*, which relate the similar words of Mother Earth (Tel-
lus) to the Sun (Apollo):

> Why do you bathe your divine face in the filthy brine?
> You will entrap coolness much better in my shadow,
> Apollo.
> Come hither, moisten your glittering locks in the dew;
> a gentler sleep will come to you in the chill grass.
> Come hither and place your rays on my bosom;
> wheresoever you lie about, a gently murmuring breeze
> will soothe
> our bodies spread on humid roses.
> A destiny like Semele's (believe me) does not frighten me,
> nor the axle smoking from Phaeton's horse.
> When you, Apollo, use your fire more wisely,
> come hither and place your rays on my bosom.
> Thus wanton Earth breathes out her loves.
>
> (ll. 84–95)

Unifying these three books of the second unit of *Paradise
Regain'd* is the new invocation of Book II, introducing the rest
of the poem, and Mary's soliloquy, completed by the final
lines of the poem. Milton cites the first disciples Andrew and
Simon Peter, who were fishermen, and as Plain Fishermen

they pray, "God of *Israel*,/Send thy Messiah forth, the time is come," and conclude, "Soon we shall see our hope, our joy return." Mary also laments Jesus's absence but is inured to wait with patience. The effect of this fresh start is to emphasize the fleeting appearance of the Messiah and his obscurity thus far, thereby to contrast with his return and his ministry to come after he has been fully prepared. The fishermen represent humankind who greets each new generation with the hope that man will be freed from his yoke by that generation's advancements, and Mary is woman—wife and mother—who waits in patience. As before, she awaits knowledge and understanding of what delays her son, "his absence now/Thus long to some great purpose he obscures."

A fish represents knowledge and wisdom; it is mythically therefore a guardian of the tree of knowledge and of the tree of life. It has become in Christian symbolism an emblem of baptism and the Holy Eucharist. And thus the Son as one sought by the fishermen is all these things symbolically. Fish is the food the Messiah will catch at the end of the world and divide among the faithful. But, too, the fish represents the sea and sea is a mother archetype, and a fish in Christian terms is also then an emblem of the Virgin Mary. The citation of Andrew and Simon Peter, who, according to Matthew 4:19, follow Jesus to become "fishers of men," indicates the Christian transference of tangible and sexual pursuits to nonmaterial and spiritual goals which the temptations of books II–IV will effect for the Son. (We should remember that Andrew and Simon Peter are not named in the Bible until after Jesus begins his ministry, that is, not until after the time sequence of Milton's poem ends. Milton's purpose in bringing them in at this point must therefore be significant: his lines derive from John 1:29–42, which deals with John the Baptist's testimony and its aftermath and which omits mention of the temptation in the wilderness.) The temptations of books II–IV first reject sexual appetite, then bodily appetite; next, the material things of life—wealth, glory, kingdom; next, the lures of knowledge; and finally the contempt for any other being—God—which might ensue in one who, having learned to reject the tangible and sexual and having adopted as values the nonmaterial and spiritual, might become vainglorious.

While normally man breaks ties with the mother by sexual activity with surrogates and by competition with the father in spheres of community, the Son rejects or has rejected for him such sensual pleasure and rejects competition with the Father in community areas; and without such competition no question of vainglory arises. The pleasure principle is sublimated into spiritual life and the competition is defeated by humility. The temptations of books II–IV represent the state of maturity described by Freud in *Totem and Taboo*, "having renounced the pleasure principle and having adapted himself to reality, he seeks his object in the outer world." For the Son the outer world is the world of men to whom his ministry, unimpeded by personal concerns, will be directed.

What I have suggested is that *Paradise Regain'd* depicts the allegory of Man's achievement of the Paradise within, first, by full knowledge and acceptance of the Self, which implies an awareness of Godhead and the Spirit of God within one, thereby assuming the energy of the Father; and, second, by rejection of the bodily, the material, the worldly as goods, which implies renunciation and passivity, thereby assuming the meekness of the mother. A kind of double initiation exists in the poem. The first is enhanced by the full break between books I and II and by the continuity of books II, III, and IV, the initiation of the Son lying in Book I and his movement into reality lying in books II–IV. The second initiation is constituted by the full poem, and the reality into which he will move lies in his ministry after the poem ends. The poem thus initiates him from being mere Man into being the Man-God. The first initiation is thus a recapitulation, symbolically, of any man's life, to be completed with the return to the womb. The second initiation is that which gestates the Man-God who will enter the real wilderness of the world after, having returned to his mother's house, he emerges from his mother's world to undertake his ministry.

It will be clear to those who know my study of the Exodus myth in *Paradise Lost* that I view the temptation in the wilder-

ness as the antitype of the exodus.[3] It is the parable by which
Man learns how to remove himself from the secured existence
of the parental—primarily maternal—home in order to face
and conquer the wilderness of life. It is the story of Stephen
Dedalus, for example, leaving mother and mother Ireland to
become the great artificer of his race. All initiation ritual
partakes of this mythopoeic exodus, the long view of which
sees man moving forward, "light after light well spent," until
Mankind is prepared to face the bright splendor of God at the
end of time. Exodus as myth represents the stages of history
through which each man and each generation go, proceeding
linearly forward (rather than cycling back in mere repetition
of the past). The close of *Paradise Regain'd* implies such for-
ward motion, and though we have not seen a future as we do
in books XI and XII of *Paradise Lost*, the implications of what
that future will be for Jesus, for Andrew and Simon Peter, and
ultimately and continuously for Man are clear. The myth of
Exodus does not allow for a climax and a living-happily-ever-
after close for a literary work—as much here as in Joyce's *A
Portrait of the Artist as a Young Man*, which title in itself disallows
such an attitude. For like Jesus, the man who proceeds to the
next stage of history does not rest but deliberately moves
outward and beyond when the next stage takes on elements of
a secured existence.

One of my stresses has been the development of male
energy and female form for that energy, and another has been
the structure of one to three in the poem. We have talked
about the concepts of one; it is symbolic of being and of the
revelation to men of the spiritual essence. Let us now look at
three, and then at the completed poem in four books.[4] The
most usual relationship of three for most of us is the Trinity,
for three has the property of order and divinity. It is also the
first male number. What occurs in books II–IV, which are

3. *With Mortal Voice*, ch. 11, pp. 119–38.

4. Cullen, *Infernal Triad* (p. 173), recognizes these numerological relationships:
"Milton chose to contain the three days of temptation within four books in order to
provide a structural version of the nature of the *deus homo* Himself: three (*deus*, the
spiritual) and four (*homo*, the corporal, the mortal)."

carefully unified though distinct, is the creation of order out of
the potential chaos that any slight succumbing to Satan's
blandishments could produce. The energy discovered in Book
I is employed throughout these three books to establish the
divinity which the Son's humiliation predicates. The ternary,
according to Plato, is the number that pertains to the idea.
The idea of *Paradise Regain'd* is the means to regain the lost
earthly paradise: Milton urges that the search is successfully
completed by rejection of avarice and pride (the two appeal-
ing arguments by which Satan wins over Eve). The ternary
involves moral and spiritual dynamics—because of its associa-
tion with Godhead—and accordingly it is the moral and
spiritual that is brought into play in books II–IV. Milton
argues that the search for the earthly paradise is successfully
completed by meekness, that is, by obedience and faith. The
seemingly passive is to become the active spirit created from
the matter of the full poem. The number three symbolizes
such creation. It is on purpose that Milton develops within a
threefold section implying maleness the female attribute of
meekness: the soul-image is achieved only by the uniting of
animus and anima.

But the poem is in four books. Here we have a strong
example of Jung's postulate that an unconscious tendency in
Christian culture has been to round off the trinitarian formula
of the Godhead with a fourth element. This fourth element
tends to be feminine and evil, for separated from Godhead it
became God's counterpart in the form of matter itself (that is,
typically, the devil or woman as temptress), but the uncon-
scious wishes reunification. Rejection of matter or temptation
will not effect reunification. And so in Christian thought the
reunification of God's counterpart with Godhead was achieved
through the feminine, but not evil, Virgin Mary. In *Paradise
Regain'd* the section defining one in contrast with the section
defining three develops the male attribute of energy while it
rejects the evil of this fourth element, matter, through re-
straint or self-control. In the section defining three, the virtue
of this fourth element, the meekness associated with the
Virgin Mary, is developed. It is the opposite of evil which

arises from nonobedience and nonfaith (nonlove); it is established and comes as a result of the achievement of Self through the presence of the unified Godhead within man. The quaternary—for which we can read the poem itself—is a symbol of integration. Milton avoids duality in the poem by his one:three structure.

The number four is associated, we remember, with humankind; it corresponds to the earth and to the material pattern of life. It implies tangible achievements. It is thus appropriate as a principle structuring the poem, since Milton is concerned with humankind, but his treatment of the substance of the epic by the one:three structure rejects the materiality which four implies. It sets forth the firm foundation (a further symbol which four connotes) upon which the Christian concept of divine justice will be attained, while making manifest that the individual must unite with the Trinity to achieve such divine justice. The quaternary for Plato was connected with the realization of the idea, and ranged against the idea of the ternary it returns us to the point that without such knowledge of Self as Book I develops, man becomes prey to all other temptation and cannot develop within himself the other virtues of prudence, justice, and fortitude; with such knowledge the realization of the idea of the regaining of Earthly Paradise is manifest. Mythological representation of the Self has consistently been fourfold—we need think only of the four symbolic beasts around the throne of God in Revelation (4:6–8): the first was like a lion, the second like a calf, the third had a face like a man, and the fourth was a flying eagle.

Paradise Regain'd presents the transcendence of the man Jesus into the Man/God Jesus; it is a blending of the conscious with the unconscious, of the animus with the anima, of the male principle with the female principle, of the Self with the godly. Jesus combines in his ministry the strength of the eagle and the gentleness of the dove, the power of the lion and the meekness of the lamb. He represents the oneness of Man and Woman, and *Paradise Regain'd* proclaims that Mankind's place of rest will be attained only by the symbolic Adam and Eve within us all going forth hand in hand.

Chapter Six

The Message of the Poem

A fundamental change in human attitude and thinking that moved humankind from a medieval world into the Renaissance and the beginning of what came to be the "modern" era was the gradual rejection of the belief that life on earth was a place of trial to prepare for eternal life in heaven. This attitude had fostered a world of subservience which rationalized social, economic, and political injustice by the phrase "this too shall pass" and had allowed human beings to see themselves not as masters of their own fate. It was largely a world of passivity, bolstered by religious concepts of a God who had foreordained people into a chain of being and who permitted ordeal to determine the worthy for the afterlife. Life was comparatively a short period of hardship to be followed by an eternity of bliss. Gradually such thinking as a general attitude began to disappear—although today it is still not fully dispersed—and what emerged was an emphasis on the now rather than the future, on humankind's ability to alter social, economic, and political structures, and, for those who have remained believers in a God, on its opportunities to fashion demonstrations of worthiness. Life had become not an ordeal but an action arena, and varying religious precepts emerged to reflect and at the same time create the multiplicity of differences that were born. The ensuing ideational struggles have sought to establish God at one end of a spectrum as all-knowing and directive through various kinds of balance between God and humans who are circumscribedly active or

at the other extreme as nonintervening in humankind's effect-
ing of its fate. (Of course, there are those "who think not God
at all" [*Samson Agonistes*, l. 295]).

Part of Milton's aim in *Paradise Lost* was to "justifie the
wayes of God to men" (I.26), where the dative noun is plural
and is thus suggestive of justification to human beings as
individuals (rather than only the generalized group "man"),
and where the preposition "to" suggests both justification of
God's ways to the understanding of humans and justification
of God's ways toward humans. The givens for Milton are a
God who is omnipotent, omnipresent, and omniscient; a God
who is loving, understanding, and merciful; but a God who
knows that humankind is weak, will fall, must take the conse-
quences once warned, and can become worthy only through
its own unassisted action. The very early paraphrase on Psalm
114 laid out Milton's belief that people must act and that once
they have moved toward worthy achievement in God's moral
world, then God will assist them out of adversities that are not
of their making. This Adam and Eve learn as the path to the
Paradise within as they leave Eden. It is path of the exile from
past bliss, whether of innocence and childhood or of the
seemingly secure life: it is a path through a wilderness of
uncertainty and potential dangers, and such rite of passage is
mythically the only path to galvanize one to the whole of life.[1]
For the believer in God, like Milton, it was the only means to
make oneself worthy.

In a major article detailing the significance of these mythic
and philosophic substructs for Milton's epic, Mother Mary
Christopher Pecheux drew the parallels between Abraham's
departure from Ur and Adam's from Paradise, established the
harmony of the exile motif with the mythic journey and quest
of the hero (humankind's setting forth on its earthly pilgrim-
age), and she elaborated the fusion of the obedience-and-faith
theme within the wandering Christian, "a pilgrim on his way
to the heavenly fatherland."[2] Such exile and wandering

1. Compare *With Mortal Voice*, pp. 119–38.
2. Mother Mary Christopher Pecheux, "Abraham, Adam, and the Theme of
Exile in *Paradise Lost*," *PMLA* 80 (1965): 365–71.

(which, of course, implies errancy) may appear aimless but "may be in fact the following of a sure way marked out by Providence" (p. 366). Through assertion of God's providence for humankind, the remainder and indeed the emphatic part of Milton's aim in his epic, Milton believed that God's love and mercy would be demonstrated. Such assertion should enter humankind's understanding and thereby justify whatever God's ways are as ultimately loving and merciful; and such demonstration should show that whatever people undergo is justified as ultimately the sure way to aid the pilgrim on his or her way to Heaven. For another given for Milton is the existence of and desire of humankind for the afterlife at the right hand of God, the return to the lost Eden, the Garden, the Golden Age, the "endless morn of light." What God has provided is the Son.[3]

Paradise Lost as Mother Christopher made clear not only is concerned with the theme of exile, but offers Milton's philosophic view of the issues behind this our life, his implication that exile and mythic journey must be undergone, and we can here note Milton's analysis of what would later be Jungian themes.[4] But counsel to render loss and human frailty into achievement and strength is also encased in the epic. To Adam's "suffering for Truths sake," a form of the malaise of the medieval world, and his "to obey is best . . . and on him [God] sole depend," a form of the passivity of the past, Michael answers,

> onely add
> Deeds to thy knowledge answerable, add Faith,
> Add Vertue, Patience, Temperance, add Love,
> By name to come call'd Charitie, the soul
> Of all the rest . . .   (XII.581–85)

3. See Shawcross, *With Mortal Voice*, pp. 21–32.

4. See also Isabel G. MacCaffrey, *Paradise Lost as "Myth"* (Cambridge: Harvard University Press, 1959).

Be active is the counsel, for even patience is doing on the part of the patient one: "They also serve who only stand and wait," Milton wrote in Sonnet 19. Such counsel is not developed in *Paradise Lost*, for Milton's subject has been "mans disobedience," and his solace for humankind is that out of such disobedience can come the realization that obedience is best, just as only through evil can its opposite, good, be known, as he etched into our consciousness in *Areopagitica*. He evinces that the dark vast abyss (whether that out there in man's world or that within himself—presented as a female womb symbol) can produce dovelike creatures (those like the Holy Spirit itself—presented as a male progenerating figure). The oppositions thus imply that exile will bring union, that suffering will bring peace, that obedience to God will bring independence of Satan. Yet the action requisite to add charity to one's makeup is not elaborated: for this poem action (or exercise of free will) has brought about its subject, disobedience. The capstone of opposing such action by an opposing exercise of free will is only stated by Michael, as contrastively in the middle of the poem Raphael had warned through the rebellious angels' example:

> let it profit thee t'have heard
> By terrible Example the reward
> Of disobedience; firm they might have stood,
> Yet fell; remember, and fear to transgress.
> (VI.909–12)

The second half of the poem details the incompleteness of Adam and Eve's heeding that warning, but heeding it would have turned largely on nonaction, a passivity to a warning involving "don't." What happens after Michael's counsel, which is not a warning but advice and which involves "do," that is, action, is shown in books XI and XII. For the readers of the poem, however, the ones to whom Milton's aim of asserting providence and justifying God's ways to men is directed, the counsel is left undeveloped: books XI and XII give examples of those on earth who have and who have not been obedient, in parallel with the angels in Raphael's account of the War in Heaven. Not even Noah's action is one that illustrates a follower of Michael's counsel, but of one whose action involves exile. Though much of the substance of *Paradise Regain'd* informs *Paradise Lost*, it is easy to see why Thomas Ellwood missed it and asked for a "Paradise found."

That Milton takes on the prophetic voice in *Paradise Lost* has often been discussed, Mother Christopher in her last published article noting that Milton "needed to envelop the whole in an aura of the supernatural, to present his poem as a revelation from on high. The role of the prophet for his epic voice accomplished these ends."[5] The prophetic voice presents a vision of a future, the "end" of which is a form of the lost Eden; takes others to the threshold of that future and lays out its path; but is unable to continue on that path or reach that future. The Mosaic voice is an archetypal rendition of the prophet, and Milton in *Paradise Lost* has taken on such a persona, "That Shepherd, who first taught the chosen Seed." The long epic points the way to afterlife with God: obedience, although it is couched in concepts of negation and resistance. However, there is also reference to and implication of the priestly role, whose counsel heals the blind men of this dark world and wide: "Go, wash in the pool of Siloam" (John 9:7). (As the Geneva Bible glosses the line, this was interpreted as a prefiguring of the Messiah.) "*Siloa*'s Brook that flow'd/Fast by the Oracle of God" (I.11–12) had been created by Hezekiah's action to thwart Sennacherib and the Assyrians by diverting the waters of Gihon Spring ("Virgin's Fountain") from outside Jerusalem into the Brook Kidron within the city (2 Kings 20:20 and 2 Chron. 32:3–14). The lesson is that action, even seemingly unnatural action like the diverting of waters from their natural flow, must be taken at times to

5. Sister Mary Christopher Pecheux, "The Council Scenes in *Paradise Lost*," in Sims and Ryken, *Milton and Scriptural Tradition*, p. 102.

defeat (or at least thwart) one's enemy. Milton's multifarious line (which has topographically descended from the top of Oreb to Sion Hill and now to within the earth itself) suggests in its extended metaphoric reading that within the human being, who was made of the red clay (*Adam*) of the earth—and Jesus had anointed the blind man's eyes with clay made of his own spittle upon the ground—is a spirituality and life, which is next to God's oracle.[6] Water has long symbolized spirituality, of course. That oracle—"the oracle of God," that is, the Son, so titled in X.182, and *Paradise Regain'd* I.460–61—can be approached by partaking of the spirituality within one's self (for man is the temple of the Spirit of God [1 Cor. 3:16]). Such an approach to the concept of the Son (to the "Oracle of God") and what he stands for—filial love, obedience, mercy, and charity—exists in *Paradise Lost* but is not its main concern. As the great argument of the epic manifests (to "assert Eternal Providence,/And justifie the wayes of God to men"), the main concern is to lead humankind to conclude with Adam "that to obey is best,/And love with fear the onely God" (XII.562–63). It is basically an Old Testament attitude, one where the Law represented for most people a covenant with God,[7] and it is understandable why the very human, postlapsarian Adam exhibits this limitation and misreading of prohibition as covenant. His belief "that suffering for Truths sake/Is fortitude to highest victorie" (XII.569–70) stresses the outward (although it need not of necessity) and is consonant with a

6. That is, of course, a New Testament reading. I might thus mention here an Old Testament lesson which is cognate with Eve's disobedience and the dialectic substruct we have mentioned for the poem. Jonathan's tasting of the honey unwittingly against his father Saul's express command not to eat any food (1 Sam. 14:27) is not unlike Eve's partaking of the fruit through fraud: for both there comes an enlightenment. But Jonathan, unlike Eve, has acted against an unwise command and so his enlightenment is good. He concludes, "How much more, if haply the people had eaten freely today of the spoil of their enemies which they found? for had there not been now a much greater slaughter among the Philistines?" (v. 30). The blind man who is enlightened by the waters of Siloam has followed a wise command. The question is, What is Right Reason? and how is it determined? and How is False Reason discerned?

7. Compare my discussion in "Milton and Covenant: The Christian View of Old Testament Theology," in Sims and Ryken, *Milton and Scriptural Tradition*, pp. 160–91.

doctrine of works, "by small/Accomplishing great things"
(XII.566–67). He has been shown examples of the worthy
and the unworthy, and reaches his conclusions

> Taught . . . by his example whom I now
> Acknowledge my Redeemer ever blest.   (XII.572–73)

But Milton's essential belief, worked into the fabric of the
poem but whose basic concern lies elsewhere, as I have said, is
that only by an inner being enlightened through the clay of
humanity and the water of spirituality will true worth appear.
Worth does not lie in the external, in works for a public arena,
in negation and prohibition, nor in a mere following of exam-
ple, no matter how blest the example may be, if the inner
being has not been enlightened.

Michael keeps saying this, but it falls on noncomprehend-
ing ears:

> Hee to his own a Comforter will send,
> . . . who shall dwell
> His Spirit within them, and the Law of Faith
> Working through love, upon thir hearts shall write,
> To guide them in all truth, and also arm
> With spiritual Armour, able to resist
> *Satans* assaults, . . .   (XII.486–92)

Significantly, Adam's ensuing remarks are followed by a
pause (for Adam has not fully understood), and "th' Angel
last repli'd" the counsel already quoted. But for Adam and
Eve their exile will be "with wandring steps and slow," and
their progeny will only seldom comprehend "Charitie, the
soul/Of all the rest."[8]

8. A thesis of Book II of *De doctrina christiana*, which is about the worship of God
and charity, is man's duty to himself, the subject of two chapters, and his duty to his

While the ostensible subject and even "plot" of *Paradise Regain'd* is iterated in the longer poem, as Harris F. Fletcher contended,[9] we know that Milton became aware of the need for the companion poem as a result of Ellwood's question put to him with the return of the manuscript of *Paradise Lost*. The poem that emerged is dedicated to a philosophic belief in a person's ability to fashion his or her worth in God's moral world and to break from the shackles of the fundamental slavery to self, world, or false idols of the mind. The emphasis was here, as we like to assign to Renaissance thought, on the individual. The individual should act within the purview of God and under the grace of God, but of oneself: the lines from Sonnet 7 come to mind. One man is portrayed in the brief epic who has learned that to obey is best, who loves the only God (though not with or out of fear), who suffers for truth's sake, and who certainly is a supreme example for humankind to follow, but he does not "on him *sole* depend." The Son/Man adds faith, virtue, patience, temperance, and even toward his or our archenemy adds charity. The Son is guided by providence as much as are Adam and Eve, and his is a solitary way; and as his ordeal begins, his wandering and slow steps have taken him to a desert, a wilderness:

> One day forth walk'd alone, the Spirit leading;
> And his deep thoughts. The better to converse

neighbor, the subject of seven of its seventeen chapters. Milton defines charity as "A GENERAL VIRTUE, INFUSED INTO BELIEVERS BY GOD THE FATHER, IN CHRIST, THROUGH THE SPIRIT. IT EMBRACES THE WHOLE DUTY OF LOVE—BOTH LOVE FOR ONESELF AND LOVE FOR ONE'S NEIGHBOR." See Maurice Kelley, ed., *Complete Prose Works of John Milton* trans. John Carey (New Haven: Yale University Press, 1973), vol. 6, p. 717.

9. "How, then, was it to be regained, except by complete obedience to God's command? . . . That is, Christ would overcome Satan simply and solely in obeying God by not obeying Satan. All this is carefully worked out in *Paradise Lost* which opens with the idea fully formed, see Book 1:1–5." See IV.10. However, it should be clear that I disagree with the reading of the brief epic as a demonstration of obedience "simply and solely," and I must remark that the Son is not yet Christ in the poem. Christ, though it equates with Messiah in one sense, implies for the Christian the Son after his crucifixion.

With solitude, till far from track of men,
Thought following thought, and step by step led on,
He enter'd now the bordering Desert wild,
And with dark shades and rocks environ'd round, . . .

                                        (I.189–94)

The all-encompassing oxymoron "Desert wild" is Milton's
way of indicating the full range of the outer and inner worlds
in which temptation may strike. That the subject of *Paradise
Regain'd* is obedience, in contrast with that of *Paradise Lost*, and
that the crux is temptation in both, not simply Satan and his
wiles, should be manifest. Just as disobedience is not the
simple and sole concern of the one poem, obedience is not the
simple and sole concern of the other. But the significance of
temptation seems to be generally ignored for the latter work,
perhaps because some readers have come to it with an under-
lying assumption that the Son cannot really be tempted at
all.[10] This has led to opinions that the poem is static; that the
integrating theme is Satan's attempt to determine whether the
Son is indeed the Son of God or, its obverse, the Son's attempt
to determine who he is; and that there is little that ordinary
humans can emulate. I have tried to deal with these misread-
ings in chapter 5, which argues the Son's psychological devel-

10. An important exception is Stanley Fish in "Things and Actions Indifferent:
The Temptation of Plot in *Paradise Regained*," in Ide and Wittreich, *Composite Orders*,
pp. 163–85. Fish makes a telling point in discussing IV.606–8, where the narrative
voice informs us that the Son has regained lost Paradise "by vanquishing/
Temptation": "But the biggest . . . surprise is the one that awaits us in line 608 when
we discover that the object of 'vanquishing' is not Satan, as the military language and
the scene just past would seem to dictate, but temptation. 'Temptation' is not only
the word we get; it correctly names our desire for the word we didn't get. That is, it is
a temptation to expect something other than (the word) *temptation*, to expect an
external object of 'vanquishing,' . . ." (p. 183). I should also remark my strong
agreement with the import of Fish's opening comments on Michael and Adam's
soliloquy in Book XII, for as I implied before in noting Michael's pause and Adam's
noncomprehension, Michael does often rebuke Adam and challenge his assumptions,
though other commentators seem not to have understood this. We should definitely
not take on all of Adam's postulations. Adam is not a spokesman, though he may
often say things with which Milton would agree: he is now postlapsarian man, with
discernment and with failings.

opment to a man of action by internalization of action, a development, of course, which answers Michael's counsel to Adam (and to Everyman). Only through an individual's fusion of the obedience-and-faith theme with selfhood can humankind achieve, Milton is saying, and thus one is worthy only when action is unassisted.[11] One does not on God *sole* depend. The brief epic, seen this way, delineates how patience and temperance are action, how they, once constituents of the inner being, are available for action outside that inner being. We should, of course, remember what happens after *Paradise Regain'd* ends: the history of the solitary life depicted in the Gospels. As the heavenly host sing as the poem ends:

Hail Son of the most High, heir of both worlds,
Queller of Satan, on thy glorious work
Now enter, and begin to save mankind.   (IV.633–65)

The stage is set for the Son's (Jesus's) action in this world, action defined by obedience, sufferance, faith, virtue, patience, temperance, and love, that is, by charity.

The temptation motif, we should note, implies a tendency to sin. Going back to its Hebraic etymological roots, Mother Christopher has analyzed the way *sin* figures in *Paradise Regain'd*, positing a twofold temptation overlying the rather standard threefold world-the-flesh-and-the-devil motif.[12] Books I and II deal with sin potentially arising from error, the rejection of which may lead to salvation through moral strength, and books III and IV, with sin potentially arising from rebellion, the rejection of which may lead to salvation through

11. I cast as the basic tragedy of life for Milton the reliance on the hope of God's intervention in times of adversity, the presumptive deputation of man's action to supernal action, rather than doing to avoid or to alter ill. Compare my essay, "Irony as Tragic Effect: *Samson Agonistes* and the Tragedy of Hope," in *Calm of Mind*, ed. Joseph A. Wittreich (Cleveland: The Press of Case Western Reserve University, 1971), pp. 289–306.

12. Mother Mary Christopher Pecheux, "Sin in *Paradise Regained*: The Biblical Background," in Wittreich, *Calm of Mind*, pp. 49–65.

intellectual perception.[13] To counter sin by error (in a more moral and bodily sense), we recognize that one must exercise obedience, faith, virtue, and/or temperance; to counter sin by rebellion (in a more intellectual sense), one must exercise patience, love, and charity, and perhaps undergo sufferance. *Paradise Regain'd* was produced to make clear, to even Milton's fit audience that had failed to understand from *Paradise Lost*, that turning back of temptation, the defeat of the Satan within us, is accomplished by making Michael's counsel a part of us, by founding within a Paradise happier far.

The "Desert wild" to which the Son is led clues the reader to interpret both aridity (which also implies a lack of spirituality) and uncontrolled fecundity (which also implies intemperance and nondirection). Satan, as aged man in rural weeds, stresses its aridity: "we here/Live on tough roots and stubs, to thirst inur'd/More then the Camel, and to drink go far" (I.338–40). But the "dew" (l. 306) and fowl (l. 501) and wild beasts (ll. 310, 502), which come forth after forty days have passed, suggest that it only appears arid, and one suspects that Satan knows this.[14] Even in such circumstances, Milton is saying, man can dig into himself to separate and make cogent the

> multitude of thoughts at once
> Awak'n'd in [him] swarm[ing]   (I.196–97)

while he

13. See Dick Taylor, "Grace as a Means of Poetry: Milton's Pattern for Salvation," *Tulane Studies in English* 4 (1954): 75.

14. Note that the narrative voice employs a simile in introducing Satan as the aged man seeking a stray ewe or gathering withered sticks to serve "Against a Winters day when winds blow keen,/To warm him wet return'd from field at Eve" (I. 317–18). The "Desert wild" seems hardly a desert except that it offers the Son no food or drink and except that it functions as metaphor. "Desert" as *desolate* does not square with "wild," and as *uninhabited* is rendered meaningless when the aged man appears (even though it is the fraudulent Satan).

consider[s]
What from within [he] feels [him] self, and hear
What from without comes often to [his] ears   (I.197–299)

The Son's thoughts reprise his formerly envisioned heroic acts and victorious deeds, the subduing and quelling of violence and tyranny; then persuasion of the stubborn by words. Mary's remembered statements that he is Messiah and should "By matchless Deeds express [his] matchless Sire" (l. 233) had moved him to await "The time prefixt" to start to attain "the promis'd Kingdom," which time comes as the Spirit descends on him at his baptism. Before the time of his move into the wilderness, then, he has entertained the usual means to show worthiness, to struggle for truth, the extent of the Adamic understanding. With the descent of the Spirit, he knows "the time/Now full, that [he] no more should live obscure,/But openly begin . . . (I.286–88). His journey into the wilderness is parallel with Abraham's and Adam's exiles of which Mother Christopher has written. It is in fact a period of transition as he leaves his parochial obscurity to begin a public life, that which will have its inception after the poem has been completed. This interim period must be solitary, punctuated only by appearances of Satan, for this exile, like all others involving the pilgrim on his or her way to the heavenly fatherland, becomes the quest to find the means to do "as best becomes/Th'Authority which [one] deriv'd from Heav'n."

What the brief epic is about is the ways in which Michael's counsel can be internalized and made available for action. For its seamless and unconditional existence within a man or woman, its force of being must be able to sally forth and meet the adversary in every possible arena, defeating that adversary by its very existence at every turn. Milton's "message" is what he came to realize politically and mundanely: one must change people, not just institutions; one must "re-form," not simply "reform." The way to alter social, economic, and political structures is to alter the people involved in them—a stupendous and regrettably manifest impossibility, although inroads may be achieved. *Paradise Regain'd* in its own way is a political document put in metaphysical terms. The way to fashion one's worthiness is to be so worthy within that all external action demonstrates that inner being. Worth is not shown by a mere following of command or maintenance of prohibition. It is by self-action.

The Son in *Paradise Regain'd* has, it seems, always been viewed as an exemplar, whom Milton is urging his faithful, God-loving reader to emulate. I think that is wrong. Raphael had warned Adam and Eve by example, and it did not work. Michael has counseled Adam, but he is taught by the example of Jesus, he says, and still the history of humankind shows that that of itself does not work either. Milton was not, I feel sure, urging man or woman to imitate, to follow example, but rather to achieve an independence of worth, a spiritual inner being, for one's essentiality is the only thing that is going to guide action when there is no precedent to follow. It is, in this regard, important to note that the Son in *Paradise Regain'd* is never offered as an example: only Mary uses the word *example*, as reported by the Son in his first soliloquy:

> high are thy thoughts
> O Son, but nourish them and let them soar
> To what highth sacred vertue and true worth
> Can raise them, though above example high . . .
> (I.229–32)

Like Adam, Mary is fully human in referring to example, but Milton has her recognize that even high example can be too low for some. The Son is not example: he is above example. The four uses of the word in *Samson Agonistes* fit the point I am suggesting: in l. 166 the Chorus calls Samson an example for others; in l. 290 Samson ironically and with scorn says to enroll him in the list of examples of Great Deliverers; and in ll.

765 and 822, speaking to Dalila, he labels himself an example (or potential example) for posterity because of his infamous actions where she has been concerned. In *Paradise Regain'd* Milton has not created the Son as an example to be imitated but as one man whose rite of passage has shown how to live one's life.[15]

While the theme of exile enters *Paradise Regain'd* with the Son's sojourn in the desert wild, it is superseded by a theme of confrontation, which will produce "one greater Man," who is by his inner being unassistedly able to resist temptation, the sin of error and rebellion, the self, the community, and supposed authority. Exile as a rite of passage or as an exodus is necessary to life, to growing up, and is enmeshed in the psyche of the world because, through observation, humans knew that normal human beings transcend physically, emotionally, intellectually into adults at an age around puberty. We begin *Paradise Regain'd* with exile, the path for the pilgrim through the dark forest of life is discovered through confrontation, and we end awaiting the ministry of Jesus to aid humankind in finding the path themselves. The fairer Paradise now found (IV.613) is what would be Adam's "Paradise within . . . happier farr" had he understood Michael's counsel. It is the inner being that each person can achieve, Milton believed (or wanted to believe); it is a Paradise that does not require ascent to an afterlife at the right hand of God. In *Paradise Regain'd* Milton took on the priestly voice counseling clay and water: take upon yourself humanity but within the great taskmaster's eye.

Another view of the message of the poem can be seen by what Robert A. Kantra has called religious satire and the

15. The temptation episode in the life of Jesus is a rendition of the mythopoeic concept of the rite of passage between youth and adulthood, culminating symbolically in the rite of confirmation. There is need for separation from the past secure world of family, a need for development of the individual as being and then as a part of a public world. *Paradise Regain'd* is the story of Jesus's initiation, and a mirror of what ours could be. It should be easily agreed that Milton's inclusion of Belial's suggestion to set women in the Son's eye and in his walk (II.153) is a necessary component of this rite of passage and a wholly decorous way of handling it for the Son of God, now man.

visual field in which it emerges.[16] "All things vain" is the verbal earmark of such satire and appropriately appears in the description of the Paradise of Fools in Book III of *Paradise Lost*. This allegoric "*Limbo* large and broad" (495) will be peopled with those whose works Sin has filled with vanity:

> Both all things vain, and all who in vain things
> Built thir fond hopes of Glorie or lasting fame,
> Or happiness in this or th' other life.   (III.448–50)

The satiric view that God holds of humankind, thus, lies in the emptiness of its endeavors and the vain expected ends of its actions, which ends are glory and fame above God. But such glory and fame are nothing in the eyes of God, who has such people in derision. A basic text for this interpretation, and indeed for *Paradise Lost* itself, is Psalm 2:1–4:

> Why do the heathen rage, and the people imagine a vain thing? The kings of the earth set themselves, and the rulers take counsel together, against the Lord, and against his Anointed, saying, Let us break their bands asunder, and cast away their cords from us. He that sitteth in the heavens shall laugh: the Lord shall have them in derision.

The satiric lies in the distance between action and its intent and people's achievement in God's world. There is nothing satiric when these coincide.

Just before Milton introduces this perception of the Paradise of Fools, which lies "o'er the backside of the World farr off," to be filled with "all these upwhirled aloft" (III.493–95), Satan is seen in Chaos: "here walk'd the Fiend at large in spacious field" (III.430). Religious satire is thus linked with

16. See Robert A. Kantra, *All Things Vain: Religious Satirists and Their Art* (University Park: Pennsylvania State University Press, 1984) for a full discussion.

the visual and, in accordance with the imagery that Milton employs, with the spatial particularly. The distance between the vain attempts of humans for glory and fame on earth and God's world defines not only the satiric, but defines it literally in spatial metaphors.

Linkage of the satiric and *Paradise Regain'd* may seem strange at first, yet the second and third temptations specifically deal with those issues of vanity clustering around wealth, glory, kingdom, assertion of one person over many, both politically and intellectually, and that most fundamental issue of vanity, the earthly being's rivalry with God. From God's point of view such endeavors are vain—with the Latin meaning of *empty* or *idle* being paramount—and Milton's brief epic recounts how one man resisted such vanity by obedience and patience, and by recognition that he did not need more wealth or glory or power in this world than he already had. This distance between the lures offered by Satan and their rejection by the Son through a firm trust in God is repeatedly expressed in spatial terms—the view of the clashing armies, the panorama of Athens and Rome, the flight to the pinnacle of the temple spire in Jerusalem.

This visual field, however, is always ironic. Psalm 2 should be recalled as the Son of God is taken up to a mountain high with "A spatious plain out stretch't in circuit wide" beneath and "Huge Cities and high towr'd, that well might seem/The seats of mightiest Monarchs" (III.254, 261–62). Through the unwitting action of Satan, the Son is now in a position analogous to the Lord's in Psalm 2, looking down at these "mightiest Monarchs." Just as the Lord has the earthly kings he beholds in derision, so may the Son have all that he sees in derision, all of which vain things are described by Satan in great detail with amplification by the narrative voice. The Son's answer to Satan's blandishments talks of the "ostentation vain" in the militarism displayed, exhibits the patience cited in John 7:6, "My time I told thee . . . is not yet come," and recalls the Providence of God, as Psalm 114 records, when the Red Sea and Jordan once were cleft to save the chosen people from Pharaoh, Satan's counterpart. The message of Psalm 114 is not different from the message of Psalm 91, that God will send his angels to uplift those who have made the Lord their habitation when evil may befall. This is, of course, the point on which the third temptation turns. The Son's answer here in Book III rejects the vanity that will lead others to translation to the Paradise of Fools. Satan's upwhirling of the Son aloft here and in other episodes of the brief epic is also a kind of analogue to what will allegorically occur to those who succumb to Satan's lures and who thus are upwhirled aloft to the Paradise of Fools, except, of course, that the Son does not succumb and Satan is ironically unaware of the meaning that his actions support. Each of these spatial visual fields that Satan creates in *Paradise Regain'd* in order to lead the Son into things vain is a satiric reminder of Psalm 2 and of the ensuing ascent, not into the Lord's heaven but into the Paradise of Fools, lying off the backside of the world, for those unable to resist things vain.

In addition to "all things vain," Milton talks of "all things transitorie" in his account of the Paradise of Fools in *Paradise Lost*. But the complexities of imagery in both epics require attention before looking at that phrase. Satan, as I have already noted, "walk'd . . . at large in spacious field" (III.430), in which this paradise is to be located. But Milton had first introduced this idea with an ironic pun on dark and light:

> Mean while upon the firm opacous Globe
> Of this round World, whose first convex divides
> The luminous inferior Orbs, enclos'd
> From *Chaos* and th' inroad of Darkness old,
> *Satan* alighted walks.   (III.418–22)

Satan, the antitype, as it were, of all the fools who will people this "paradise," is punningly presented as contrast to the darkness into which he has come. Elsewhere are inferior orbs which nonetheless are luminous, while this which "seems a boundless Continent" is but "Dark, waste, and wild, under the frown of Night/Starless expos'd." The play of metaphoric darkness now alighted into darker darkness gives us a visual field satirizing perception, or rather false perception, for the only "glimmering air" that allows such gradation of light comes "from the wall of Heav'n/Though distant farr" yielding "som small reflection" (III.419–29). A form of the pun is continued in the simile of a vulture from the snowy ridge of a mountain in the Himalayas, which descends on hills to gorge, then flies off to Indian streams, but first "in his way lights on the barren plains/Of *Sericana*." The vulture, or Satan, leaving the snowy ridge, like Satan swooping down from the heavens as this book of the poem ends, engorges itself on "the flesh of Lambs or yeanling Kids" just as Satan will consume the innocents of this world. The vulture lights on the barren plains, "So," writes Milton, "on this windie Sea of Land, the Fiend/Walk'd up and down alone bent on his prey' (see III.431–41). This repetition of Satan's walking up and down, alone in this visual field now untrod (III.497), is clearly a direction for the reader to remember the beginning of the Book of Job (1:7), which I have commented upon in chapter 1. As Milton casts his mind over all recorded history—and the Bible represented a version of history for him—he sees the Job story and the assault on Adam and Eve in analogous terms. Here as the Paradise of Fools is to be introduced we are to remember the Adversary challenging God that Job cannot be subject to all manner of Satan's power without his submitting. In parallel, Satan will be assaulting Adam and Eve, toward which end he "lights" on the top of Niphates as Book III of *Paradise Lost* ends (III.742).

But further parallel is seen in *Paradise Regain'd*, for here is another person to be assaulted by Satan, another person whom he attempts to reduce to things vain. The scene with its alleys brown that open in the midst of a wood in which Satan appears "As one in City, or Court, or Palace bred' (II.300), as the second temptation encounter is about to begin, is a "shade/High rooft and walks beneath" (II.293). The visual field we are presented with does not have the benefit of the light of God to dispel the *shade* and it offers *walks* such as we,

remembering the account in Job and *Paradise Lost*, might
suppose Satan traverses. It is one of only eight uses of the
word *walk* in any form in the brief epic. Another is contrastive
with this usage, occurring as the second temptation ends and
the third is being prepared for, thus framing the extended
account of the second temptation. (Five uses appear before the
temptation begins and the remaining instance significantly
describes Athens and its "studious walks and shades" [IV.
243], in the midst of the lure of *contemplativa*.) This contrastive
usage has Satan discovering Jesus after the storm scene,
"walking on a Sunny hill," which is "back'd on the North and
West by a thick wood." (Milton's loaded metaphorical lan-
guage is always amazing. Here "back'd" recalls for us the
Paradise of Fools on the backside of the world, and the
geographic directions play upon the North as the cold and
unsunned quarters of the Satanic host and upon the West as
death and the dying of the light. Jesus is, of course, the
Morning Star.) The satiric in the poem is manifest when we
observe these ironic uses of language and metaphor, one from
the perspective of the monarchs of this world, the other from
the perspective of God.

The phrase "all things transitorie" (*PL* III.446) has partic-
ular reference in *Paradise Regain'd*. The Paradise of Fools,
peopled, contrasts with Satan's walking up and down alone.
These fools will fly "from the earth/Up hither like Aereal
vapours . . . Of all things transitorie and vain, when Sin/With
vanity [has] filld the works of men" (III.444–47). Important
is the lack of real substance and weight in these works of men,
again seen as the satiric distance between humans' evaluation
and God's. Equally important is the contrast between the
transitoriness of men's works inspired by Sin and the eternali-
ties of works resultant from the human's actions filled with a
love of God. For Milton, love of God predicated faith and
obedience and therefore patience, as I have remarked. The
import of the second and third temptations, and most as-
suredly in Milton's treatment of them, is such love of God.
Underlying Milton's disregard of the works of men in the
usual sense and in the usual evaluation in the community's

view is his belief that the Law (that is, the Mosaic Law of the Old Testament) is to be acknowledged as both a representation of the covenant of grace and as works by which man can manifest his obedience to God.[17] Works that do not exhibit such obedience do not relate to the Law and cannot be construed as factors of weight and substance or signs of one's candidacy for eternal life with God. These transitory things may be observed in the visual field of such vapors as here referred to, even by their highlighting in the "glimmering air less vext with tempest loud," and most revealingly in the conjured storm the Son is to experience "After his aerie jaunt" (IV.402). The spatial metaphor of the satiric visual field is thus one where the act that takes place within it can be either transitory (if imbued with nonobedience) or eternal (if imbued with faith). Satan himself is made to categorize the lures of the second temptation as transitory, and we know, recalling the Paradise of Fools, that such transitory things are the result of Sin's filling the works of men with vanity. Satan's ironic words are: "Therefore let pass, as they are transitory, the Kingdoms of this world" (IV.209), which again has as its intertext Psalm 2. The recognition and rejection of these transitory things, and these vain things, is the burden of *Paradise Regain'd* and becomes part of the message of the poem.

The final temptation is therefore the most revealing and the most summary: here Jesus has been borne "through the Air sublime/Over the Wilderness and o're the Plain," the scenes of the first and part of the second temptations. Like the mountain to which he had been transported in Book III, with its "spatious plain" below and its cities and towers "that well might seem/The seats of mightiest Monarchs," the "glorious Temple rear'd/. . . far off appearing like a Mount/Of Alabaster, top't with Golden Spires," extending into the air above "fair *Jerusalem,*/The holy City" with its towers high. Jesus is set "on the highest Pinacle" (see IV.548–50), "highest plac'd" for "highest is best." This is "thy Fathers house," Satan tells the Son, meaning that the temple is the place of

17. See Shawcross, "Milton and Covenant," p. 167.

worship of God, but analogizing this highest locus, which extends into the air above the land, as a representation of God's heavenly abode. Remembering again Psalm 2—as well as the temple's gloriousness and golden splendor—we can see that the Son might have Satan and the monarchs below in derision, but he does not take this attitude: he remains faithful and unanxiety-ridden and nonpresumptuous, and he thus replies ambiguously, "Tempt not the Lord thy God." The ambiguity lies not in the Son's meaning but in the meaning the reader interprets from "the Lord thy God": he is God the Father, omnipotent, omniscient, and particularly now omnipresent as Jesus means the phrase, and he is God the Son, who is Jesus, and who demonstrates his divinity by his rejection of Satan's proudful temptation (cf. IV.580).

The satiric distance is emphasized. Satan acts and intends from a perspective of transitory and vain things, implying that challenge to God will lead to a kind of glory and fame and to circumstances that will bring happiness for the challenger. Jesus acts by not acting and by giving up any possible personal intentional aims to the "strong motion" that led him into the wilderness in the first place. That experience, which is now at an end with his admonition, "Tempt not the Lord thy God," he commented upon thus:

> to what intent
> I learn not yet, perhaps I need not know;
> For what concerns my knowledge God reveals.
> (I.290–94)

The tower temptation posits "all things eternal and humble with which love of God can fill the works of men" against the transitory and vain, provoked by Sin. Humankind's perspective on such acts and intentions either expands or collapses the satiric distance between.

The visual field that we behold as we are presented with the Son on the highest pinnacle of the world depends upon our perspective as well. Do we see a human being who has risen to such great height in God's spatial world that he can take upon himself authority—the perspective as we look up? Or do we see a human being who recognizes his precarious position and dependency upon "Th' Authority which one derives from Heav'n" (I.289)?—the perspective as we look down with the Son. In his opening soliloquy Jesus talks of his human intentions as a child "to do/What might be publick good," "to promote all truth/All righteous things," and of the admiration his actions brought. But he aspired further, to "victorious deeds/. . ., heroic acts,/. . . to subdue and quell o're all the earth/Brute violence and proud Tyrannick pow'r,/Till truth were freed, and equity restor'd" (I.203–20). The narrative of *Paradise Regain'd* is the alteration of that kind of perspective looking up at the admired human being to the perspective that even after we have emulated such heroic action more meaningful heroic action is available through faith and love, even when it means inaction. These are the "deeds/Above heroic," Milton proposes, even "though in secret done" (I.14–15). They do not need the acknowledgment of others since they are eternal. The acknowledgment of others, like the admiration the very human Jesus was accorded as a child, is but transitory, built upon "fond hopes of glorie or lasting fame" as they may be. Like the kings of the earth in Psalm 2, humankind strives to become independent of everything and everyone, but, Milton warns, that means to break asunder the bands of the Lord and his Anointed.

Chapter Seven

The Genre

THE definition of genre under which I write and which I firmly contend must be acknowledged to rid us of the critical confusion that so often surrounds generic discussion—such as the confusion concerning the difference between tragedy and the tragic, or satire and the satiric—is dependent upon a literary work's form, structure, and characteristics, and its author's intent toward that work.[1] It emphatically does not indicate anything about the author's intent toward the subject matter. The genre has nothing to do with the author's "philosophy" or "political persuasion" or "critical stance," although some genres are more appropriate to certain matter and attitudes than others. Genre itself implies attitude toward content, the epic, for example, implying an attitude in the content which has broad significance for humankind (rather than merely personal) and a sweep beyond the boundaries of the work itself.

The structure, form, and characteristics of epic have been examined extensively, most evidence of description coming from specific "epics"—the *Iliad*, the *Odyssey*, the *Aeneid*, to begin with. Later epics are often ranged against these three classical works, leading to such arguments as whether the *Divina Commedia* is or is not an epic. *Paradise Lost*'s relation-

---

1. See John T. Shawcross, "Literary Revisionism and a Case for Genre," *Genre* 18 (1985): 413–34.

ship to this kind of epic has, of course, been pursued, but little
has been explored for *Paradise Regain'd* in comparison. Gener-
ally accepted are the following epic earmarks: the structure of
an epic implies a series of episodes and adventures of or
concerned with a central figure over a period of time, thus
producing a lengthy poem. These episodes and adventures
intertwine, usually in a nonchronological order, particularly
having begun *in medias res*, using flashback (to use the older
term) or accounts of things past, or using *prolepsis* and building
on the device of simultaneity of action. The form depends on
the antagonistic force set against the central figure. The
episodes and the chronology, the number, type, and treatment
of other figures, and the need for contrast, comparison, or
verbal motifs will create a form that is simpler or more
complex, straightforward or integrated by repetition and jux-
tapositions, and internalizing or creating expansiveness. The
Iliad and the *Odyssey*, for the most part, represent these two
extremes of form: the *Odyssey* in a sense is simpler and expan-
sive, with at least a surface straightforwardness—man in his
social world; the *Iliad* is more complex, integrated by subtle
repetitions and psychological contrasts, and concerned with
the inner man. Characteristics of the epic are tempered by the
form, but there is a vastness in the setting, action drawn from
deeds of valor and courage, and a significance for man,
whether nation, race, or humankind. In classical epic there
are supernatural forces at work, invocation of a muse, cata-
logs, and high style and decorum; speeches are formalized,
the theme is stated explicitly, and verbal tags (repeated simi-
les, for example) abound. In descent from classical epic,
certain kinds of episodes persist, such as epic games, a descent
into hell, a battle between hero and antagonist. Further, the
epic, because of its length, vastness, complexity, and public
significance, subsumes other genres, styles, and modes (thus
making epic genre *genera mixta* and epic mode *mixed modes*).[2]

2. See Roger Rollin's discussion of "*Paradise Lost*: 'Tragical-Comical-Historical-
Pastoral,'" *Milton Studies* 5 (1973): 3–37. The elements of romance which may be
subsumed (and which distinguish romance from epic) include nonrealistic narratives
and characters, such as knights errant; deliberate placement in a time past which is

Like *Paradise Lost*, *Paradise Regain'd* is called simply "A Poem" on its title page. A well-known section of *The Reason of Church-Government* (the preface to Book II) sets up labels for the poems by discussing the "diffuse epic" and the "brief epic," with the Book of Job as example of the latter. Barbara K. Lewalski has examined *Paradise Regain'd* as brief epic on the model of Job in terms of conception and structure.[3] An insistence on an active "military" hero, a beginning *in medias res*, epic devices and verbal echoes, a declaration of intention, a council in heaven and two "infernal" councils, and prophecy of victory all place the poem as epic. Aside from its shorter length and concentration of materials (story, action, characters, and so forth) so that it does not become "diffuse," the poem exhibits strict rules regarding structure and the unities: basically an episode constitutes the whole subject, and the single combat of the hero and his antagonist, the epitome and climax of the more usual epic, becomes the whole subject. Herein lies the essence of its being a brief epic. The unified action, place, and time are most noteworthy, with basically only one action with multiple parts, various locales but all tied to the developing action, and a short period of time for the total action, apparently three days. What little of the past needs to be known is filled in by two soliloquies, the Son's in Book I and Mary's in Book II; what little is needed to anchor the subject in religious history is given by the narrator at the outset of books I and II, by the talk in the heavenly and infernal councils, and by the dialogue generated by Satan as he tries to evaluate the Son and the rumors that have whirled about him. The formal recital of history, that is, is transformed, and analogous episodes are eschewed.[4] The whole is

viewed through a scrim; digressions that are not treated as integral episodes (the possible source of Milton's extended similes which, however, are integrated into the whole); and extravagancies of story and imagery—the marvelous (which Milton turns into ironies—they never adhere to God).

3. Lewalski, *Milton's Brief Epic*.

4. Lewalski sees Belial's speech as offering an analogous episode, which, of course, is not pursued in the basic action, thus emphasizing Milton's transformation and nonemployment of a staple of the diffuse epic. The nature of the history on which the episode is conceived is likewise significant: "Like *Paradise Lost*, *Paradise Regain'd* is

not diffuse and is concentrated. Further, there is a deemphasis on typology and the supernatural, with no allegoric personifications or psychomachia. Typological symbolism is not superimposed but made to function dramatically as part of the temptation dialogue. The single combat that constitutes the subject becomes the symbol of the perpetual battle of the Son (that is, of man) and Satan through all time. The emphasis on unity and concentration within the poem has created a bareness of style (easily recognized by comparison with *Paradise Lost*), which William Riley Parker explained "in terms of dramatic models, in terms of decorum."[5]

Donald L. Guss was not entirely happy with the definition of brief epic which Lewalski culled from the tradition and previous criticism and had so greatly extended and developed. His definition of the genre is: "an historical narrative of great personages and events, evoking marvel by presenting a supreme example of virtue."[6] I take it that his unhappiness lay in the presentation of definition, which is not approached as definition, and in the source of much comment being a parade of relatively short poems on religious themes, not all of which are epical, let alone epics. Guss stresses the difference of *Paradise Regain'd* from the epic and particularly from *Paradise Lost*: the lack of magnificence, the lack of cosmological surveys, the lack of martial episodes, the lack of public oratory, the emphasis on character rather than deed, the eschewing of elaboration and turning away from that which is grand, and

---

conceived as a heroic poem grounded upon a true event; it is not a romance. In the brief epic, however, the romance allusions do not revalue the romance ethos so much as exalt it to the order of perfection." See her essay, "Milton's Revaluation of Romance," in *Four Essays on Romance*, ed. Herschel Baker (Cambridge: Harvard University Press, 1971), p. 70. On the other hand, Annabel Patterson, after having reviewed romance theory, Milton's ideas about romance, and its influence on his work, discusses the presence of Eroticism, the Matter of France, and the Marvellous in *Paradise Regain'd*, and she concludes that Milton rejects the reform of romance from within and maintains a stance "conceptually somewhere between natural and supernatural" ("*Paradise Regain'd*: A Last Chance at True Romance," in Ide and Wittreich, *Composite Orders*, pp. 187–208).

5. Parker, *Milton: A Biography*, vol. 2, p. 1142.

6. Donald L. Guss, "A Brief Epic: *Paradise Regain'd*," *Studies in Philology* 68 (1971): 223–43.

the plain form and direct style. It is this latter consideration
that he pursues as a positive characteristic of the brief epic.
"Such a style is plain and weighty without being Senecan. Its
individual figures, though perhaps not its total effect, are
Biblical. Ellipses, coordination, and epigrammatic phrasing
make for a packed style; short phrases, verbal repetitions, and
parallelism add weight; repetition of the same content in a
series of short phrases yields a somber majesty."[7] This biblical
style is seen thus in the distich and in the rhetoric with its
contrasted words arranged antithetically and its repetitive
meanings given in different words.

Prior to Lewalski's work, Stewart A. Baker turned his
attention to the problem of the genre of *Paradise Regain'd*,
although his views were not available for consultation when
Lewalski was engaged in writing and publishing her study.
Baker sees the brief epic as a distinct literary form reaching its
apogee in Sannazaro's *De partu virginis* and Milton's poem.[8]
The genre arose, Baker concludes, from a desire to reconcile
elements of the classical epic to the personal, moral, and
didactic interests of the New Testament and hagiological
materials. Its style and structure result from the unheroic and
disjointed sequence of Gospel narratives, being thus suitable
to meditation and moral debate. It is a middle style, lying
between the temperate, didactic style of Jesus and the highly
colored rhetorical style of Satan. The metaphor of the Chris-
tian soldier allows the unmilitary, moral hero the stature of
the epic military hero, Baker argues, exalting by contrast and
inversion his moral heroism. The brief epic is therefore one
employing objective epic motifs in an absolute moral frame-
work, centering upon a brief but significant episode from the
hero's career. Its aim is to interpret that career and position in
universal Christian history; its strategy lies in meditative
soliloquies, didactic orations, scenes of debate, and prophecy.

7. Ibid., p. 240.
8. See Stewart A. Baker, "The Brief Epic: Studies in the Styles and Structure of
the Genre of *Paradise Regained*" (Ph.D. diss., Yale University, 1964). An abstract was
published in *Dissertations Abstracts, International* 32 (1971): 1464A. See also his "San-
nazaro and Milton's Brief Epic," *Comparative Literature* 20 (1968): 116–32. Lewalski
considers Sannazaro's poem in *Milton's Brief Epic* on pp. 60–61.

In a revised form of a major article on the meditative dimension of the poem, Louis L. Martz stresses its didactic nature and merges it with the form and style of Vergil's *Georgics*.[9] He cites Charles Dunster's label, "the *brief*, or didactic, epic,"[10] and suggests a kind of parallelism between *Paradise Lost/Aeneid* and *Paradise Regain'd/Georgics*. "*Paradise Regain'd* shows the Son in his second, his internal function. Through a process of renunciation *Paradise Regain'd* gradually reveals the voice of Truth speaking within the illuminated mind."[11] Anthony Low includes in his analysis of the presence of georgic in the work of British Renaissance authors a review of the georgic mode in Milton's poem. "The georgic images that frame *Paradise Regained* are reinforced by recurrent georgic themes throughout the poem,"[12] he writes, labeling it a "heroic georgic" (p. 352), an essentially new genre, because of its predominantly georgic mode and heroically georgic theme.

9. Louis L. Martz, "*Paradise Regain'd*: The Interior Teacher," in Louis L. Martz, *Poet of Exile: A Study of Milton's Poetry* (New Haven: Yale University Press, 1980), ch. 15, pp. 247–71. The chapter was previously printed in *The Paradise Within: Studies in Vaughan, Traherne, and Milton* (New Haven: Yale University Press, 1967), ch. 4, pp. 171–201, a revision of his "*Paradise Regain'd*: The Meditative Combat," *ELH* 27 (1960): 223–47. See also app. 1 to *Poet of Exile*, "*Paradise Regain'd* and the *Georgics*," pp. 293–304.

10. Charles Dunster, ed., *Paradise Regained, a Poem, in Four Books* (London, 1795), p. 2n. He anticipated the tenor of recent criticism: "The Book of Job, which I have before supposed to have been our Author's model, materially resembles [*Paradise Regain'd*] in this respect [a conclusion which rises in dignity and sublimity, thereby exciting the attention and admiration of the reader], and is perhaps the only instance that can be put in competition with it. . . . They who talk of our Author's genius being in the decline when he wrote his second poem, and who therefore turn from it, as from a dry prosaic composition are, I will venture to say, no judges of poetry. With a fancy such as Milton's it must have been more difficult to forbear poetic decorations than to furnish them; and a glaring profusion of ornament would, I conceive, have more decidedly betrayed the *poeta senescens*, than a want of it. . . . The *PARADISE REGAINED* has something of the didactic character; it teaches not merely by the general moral, and by the character and conduct of its hero, but has also many positive precepts every where interspersed. It is written for the most part in a style admirably condensed, and with a studied reserve of ornament: it is nevertheless illuminated with beauties of the most captivating kind" (pp. 266–67n).

11. Martz, "Interior Teacher," p. 247.

12. Anthony Low, *The Georgic Revolution* (Princeton: Princeton University Press, 1985), p. 333. See ch. 7, "Milton and the Georgic Ideal," pp. 296–352, and esp. pp. 322–52.

The critical analyses of the poem summarized in the fore-
going paragraphs (which at times offer more definition than
their original statements provided) are certainly correct and
instructive of a good understanding of Milton's achievements
in *Paradise Regain'd*. What bothers me in all of that is that little
attention is paid to the genre brief epic except as *Paradise
Regain'd* exhibits what characteristics will then be used to
define that genre. We need a *definition* that will apply to a
family of poems called *brief epic*, not a definition (or descrip-
tion, really) of one particular member of that family. Are all
brief epics didactic, as Dunster wrote? Are all brief epics
concerned with specific moral issues and virtue, and reli-
giously oriented? Are all brief epics necessarily historical? Are
all brief epics written in a plain (and biblical) style or a middle
style? Stuart A. Curran warns us that no expectation of the
diffuse epic is omitted in the brief epic *Paradise Regain'd* except
its diffuseness:

> The brief epic is not a scale model but a concentrated form
> of its grander counterpart; and just as it tends to turn in
> upon itself in shape, so, too, there is a comparable inter-
> nalization of idea. The struggle between good and evil,
> which is the basic component of all epics, becomes cen-
> tered in a single individual representative of man, and
> from his internal conflict emerges the scope of human life,
> its triumphs and limitations.[13]

It is this kind of definition of brief epic that we need: a
definition in terms of form, structure, characteristics, and
authorial attitude (the external and the internal forms of a
genre) which will be useful in discussing, say, the poems of the
Romantics which Curran's examinations suggest (like Robert
Southey's *Thalaba the Destroyer*) or the narrative poems of
Edwin Arlington Robinson (like *Merlin*).

13. Stuart A. Curran, "The Mental Pinnacle: *Paradise Regained* and the Romantic
Four-Book Epic," in Wittreich, *Calm of Mind*, p. 136.

Accordingly, I suggest the following definition of the brief epic, building upon the concepts reviewed before: it is a poetic narrative, perhaps divided into a few (three to seven?) sections or books and totaling, perhaps, something like one to three thousand lines. It depicts one episode in the life of a central figure within a circumscribed period of time, presented ostensibly in chronological order; it may seem to begin *in medias res* (though it does not) by being drawn out of the hero's full life, that which is pertinent from the past being filled in by short accounts given by characters or the narrative voice. (It is possible, we should note, that the "central figure" could be a group treated as an individual, the episode being a timed section out of its fuller existence. However, the complexities that could arise make this generally unlikely for the brief epic.) Its meter is not different from that of the long epic and thus may be traditionally hexameter or blank verse, or less traditionally rhymed verse, so-called free verse, or mixed writing (including stanzaic forms, patterned and nonpatterned meters, or prose).[14] Because the subject of the narrative is one episode, intertwining of story or character elements is minimal and simultaneity of action is greatly reduced, but both intertwining and simultaneity will exist clearly and immediately in relationship with the central figure or the episode. The settings (if more than one) are few. While vastness and cosmological significance may exist in the brief epic, the panoramic vision and sense of man's relation to the space of nature are given smaller compass, with the central figure constantly as the focus. Such characteristics as invocations, catalogs, encyclopedic knowledge, explicit statement of theme and intention, verbal tags and epic devices, prophecy in terms of either the afterward or the public significance arising from the deeds of valor and courage—all may appear and probably do in some form. Aside from the length and lessening of complexities of story, characters, place, and time, the brief epic distinguishes itself by constantly foregrounding the

14. As examples for the long epic I think of Joel Barlow's *The Columbiad* in heroic couplets, Hart Crane's *The Bridge* in "free verse," and William Carlos Williams's *Paterson* in mixed writing.

central figure and thereby creating internalization of the action. (Those who find books V through VI and XI through XII generally excrescences of *Paradise Lost* are, of course, looking at that long epic as one that should constantly foreground Adam and Eve, as if the poem were not a diffuse epic; for them apparently it is a poem on Adam and Eve and the Fall, rather than a poem on the losing of Paradise.) Internalization may create a greater emphasis on character than on deed, as in *Paradise Regain'd*, but the brief epic as genre does not as a necessity for classification reduce deeds. Likewise there may be a greater emphasis on speech than on narration, as in *Paradise Regain'd* (the verbal debate here engaging the "military" and battle of protagonist and antagonist), but the brief epic as genre does not as necessity for classification demand this imbalance. The significance of any epic—long (diffuse) or brief—lies in the struggle between good and evil for a public audience which is represented by the central figure. The antagonist may be more than one person, may even be a "force."

The preceding defines brief epic as genre, rejecting as part of that definition certain concepts that commentators have advanced because they are exhibited in *Paradise Regain'd*. The definition fits *Paradise Regain'd* and thus further suggests that all brief epics are not necessarily historical: a brief epic may be historical but not all brief epics are historical. As epic, the brief epic should offer mixed genres, mixed modes, and mixed styles. As an earmark of genre, the style of *Paradise Regain'd* that has been described variously by critics has no pertinency. *Paradise Regain'd* does indeed show mixed genres—the hymn, the ode, the dramatic dialogue and the soliloquy, the philosophical poem, the pastoral among them; mixed modes—the tragic and the comic and the georgic; and mixed styles, as Guss's and Baker's discussions suggest. While there is a bareness in comparison with *Paradise Lost* (which exhibits high, middle, and falsely high styles) and *Samson Agonistes* (a high style that is very different from that in most of *Paradise Lost* because it is fully in human speech), the style of *Paradise Regain'd* intermixes high and middle and plain styles (that is, if we look at middle and plain as being different). The concentration of the brief epic and the reduction of those elements making for complexities will alter the tone and feeling from what they would have been in the diffuse epic, but a specific style is not necessarily attached to the brief epic that is any different from the style of the diffuse epic. The differences among the three major poems of Milton in these regards should be attributed to other reasons, not to genre.

Chapter Eight

The Poem as Sequel and as Companion

THE title of the poem discussed in this book immediately sounds like a sequel to *Paradise Lost*. "Sequel" implies that which follows upon something else, developing ideas found in the first, completing whatever has been left without full termination in the earlier, constituting a next stage in whatever the first has presented. In the case of literary works one expects similar topics, similar techniques and style, and a kind of imitation of the first—often in this regard making the latter seem lesser in the judgment of the reader (as, unfortunately, Shakespeare's *2 Henry IV* is usually viewed in comparison with *1 Henry IV*). But these two poems also set up for most readers, following the kind of thinking that Ellwood showed and that Milton acceded to, a companionship whereby the second complements the first by illustrating or discussing a way of reversal of the developed movement of the first, and by implicitly highlighting aspects of the first otherwise potentially overlooked. The second as companion fills in that which seems wanting in the first, making the two together a more complete literary work. *Paradise Lost* and *Paradise Regain'd* can be viewed as originally sequel but also as companion poems; *Paradise Regain'd* and *Samson Agonistes*, published together in the same volume in 1671, offer concepts of companion works, complementarity, and together a sequel volume to the volume *Paradise Lost*.

Others' overviews of the three major works have delineated
a pattern of *Paradise Regain'd* and *Samson Agonistes* as com-
panion poems and as developments out of *Paradise Lost/Para-
dise Regain'd*—but I would say the 1671 volume whole—func-
tions as sequel by establishing the way of return to Paradise
that was too often missed in *Paradise Lost*; that is, through the
"Paradise within." It acts as companion to that poem by
implicitly offering what has too often been read as lacking in
it, "Paradise found"; and again, that is, through the "Para-
dise within." It consciously falls into a "family" associated
with *Paradise Lost* in epical qualities and metrics, but it is its
own individual member, rendering those qualities and those
metrics different. Joseph Wittreich discussed the way in which
Paradise Regain'd interprets *Paradise Lost*, and then in turn how
Samson Agonistes interprets *Paradise Regain'd*.[1] Mary Ann Rad-
zinowicz made the relationship particularly clear in remark-
ing that in the conclusion of *Paradise Lost* "two themes for
future treatment are explicit . . .: the example of the 'Re-
deemer ever blest' and his version of heroic fortitude, and the
addition of human deeds to faith, virtue, patience, temper-
ance, and love in proportion to the knowledge of God given to
any man."[2] Wittreich parts company with many commenta-
tors on *Samson Agonistes* (for example, as he himself notes, with
Arnold Stein's view that the hero of each poem "presents a
human and individual way to the same truth"[3]) when he calls
it a warning or negative example, thus stressing Samson's fall
prior to the beginning of the work and the action required to
nullify or reverse that negativity.[4] Like others, Wittreich does
not see Samson as a type of Christ but rather as ordinary man,
Christ's opposite type, who must undergo the internal trials
that Samson does in order to be renovated. Samson, contrast-
ing with the Son of *Paradise Regain'd*, is "a hero binding men

1. Joseph Wittreich, *Visionary Poetics: Milton's Tradition and His Legacy* (San Mar-
ino: Huntington Library, 1979), pp. 191–92 and ff. See also his full study *Interpreting
Samson Agonistes* (Princeton: Princeton University Press, 1986).

2. Radzinowicz, *Toward "Samson Agonistes"*, p. 229. See also her discussion of the
poems as complementary works, pp. 227–60.

3. Stein, *Heroic Knowledge*, p. 205.

4. Wittreich, *Visionary Poetics*, p. 268 n. 295.

down to the cycles of history."[5] This accords with my own view of the poem, approached from a totally different angle. I have previously argued that the real tragedy of *Samson Agonistes* lies in our recognition as the poem ends "that Samson's story is constantly played through time and that we are part of another recurrence."[6] The wisdom of putting these two works together in the same volume is the commerce which is thus established between them: we see in Samson what the Son as Man could have become had he succumbed to any of the temptations of Satan, and in the Son we see what Samson as the "great Deliverer"—the ironic earthly counterpart of the true "heavenly" deliverer—should have been. Perhaps we have misread *Samson Agonistes* so ineptly in the past because we have not fully acknowledged the interrelationships of the two works,[7] seeing the second as a kind of *King Lear* in which the title hero's "fall" has really occurred before the opening of the play, a fall made visible in his incomprehensible division of his kingdom as it begins. Samson is not Lear, although he has fallen before the opening of the dramatic poem; he is rather, to appropriate Wittreich's word, a negative Christ.

The publication of *Paradise Regain'd* and *Samson Agonistes* in the same volume in 1671 presents us with companion pieces, regardless of their dates of original composition and revision. It is generally assumed that Milton had purpose in yoking the two, although one might entertain the thought that, in his apparent move to publish what items he had developed, he placed these two together somewhat incidentally or that the publisher proposed making an otherwise 166-page volume a 220-page one by the addition of the dramatic poem. The title page allows for whatever sales advantage a comparison with

5. Ibid., p. 207.
6. John T. Shawcross, "Irony as Tragic Effect: *Samson Agonistes* and the Tragedy of Hope," in Wittreich, *Calm of Mind*, p. 293. Further, "Samson is man fallen, man tempted, man regenerated, man saved. Samson *agonistes* is a player on the stage of the world in the endless drama of life which goes on and on in successive acts" (p. 294).
7. I think of Douglas Bush's comment that Milton "did not, certainly, have Samson's overwhelming sense of having betrayed God's cause . . ., but he had known the despair of witnessing the wreck of his and other men's hopes and labors for the nation" (*The Complete Poetical Works of John Milton* [Boston: Houghton Mifflin, 1965], p. 515).

Paradise Lost would achieve, whether only the first or both poems were included. The phrase "To which is added" on the title page may have been the printer's. A mere "and" would have looked odd on that particular title page; "together with" is a possibility, placing *Samson Agonistes* on a more equivalent status. "To which is added" has a tone making *Samson Agonistes* a lesser work, and thus sounding like the printer's means of emphasizing *Paradise Regain'd* further. Yet *Samson* is not lost on the title page, and its own title page with separate pagination for the poem implies a twofold, balanced volume, similar to Sir Thomas Browne's 1658 *Hydriotaphia Together With The Garden of Cyrus*. While the title page design and wordage may not be Milton's, the publishing of the two works in one volume can be assigned, I believe, to Milton's decision. That decision was dependent, it will be argued, upon the contrasting genres of the two works and the implications of those genres, as well as the modes and substance of the works. One poem comments upon and illuminates the other, once their genres and modes are understood.

The contrasting genres of these works are: a poem with much dialogue cast as an epic form, a poem fully in speech cast as a dramatic form.[8] Milton called *Samson Agonistes* a dramatic poem, not a drama or play and not a tragedy. The critical argument over its classification has very often ignored definition; critics in consecutive sentences have labeled it "a tragedy" and a "dramatic poem," as if these were undifferentiated and the same.[9] Some even use the word "play." Most critics seem to treat it as a play. But Milton is subtly directing his readers to understand *Paradise Regain'd* the epic as a public form presenting a central figure of heroic proportions whose actions reveal important concerns (and thought) for humankind and *Samson Agonistes* the dramatic poem as a public form

8. Richard D. Jordan, in "*Paradise Regained*: A Dramatic Analogue," *Milton Quarterly* 12 (1978): 65–68, suggests that the poems were seen as companion pieces by Milton because both are related to biblical drama. Jordan sees *Paradise Regain'd* as being in the tradition of Jean Michel's *Le Mystère de la Passion*. Comparisons of the two works are explored by Wittreich in *Interpreting Samson Agonistes*, see esp. pp. 348–62.

9. See "The Genres of *Paradise Regain'd* and *Samson Agonistes*," in Ide and Wittreich, *Composite Orders*, pp. 233–39.

presenting a figure of human proportions whose actions reveal the actions of the (typical) individual human and the potential actions of the (untypical) individual human. As poem, emphasizing its generic relationship and ignoring its form, *Samson Agonistes* allows for internalizations that can produce a character finally capable of a positive action (or of thought which may predicate action).

But the modes of these two poems have been little attended to: the first is comic; the second, tragic. Patrick Cullen, writing of the design of the poems as companion pieces, shows that they provide "a Christian definition of the two great poetic modes, the heroic and the tragic."[10] Heroic (or epic) mode does not necessitate that a work be "comic" or "tragic," and indeed the epical would subsume both effects in some way. In *Paradise Regain'd* that heroic mode subtends both the tragic potentiality which succumbing to temptation would bring and the comic potentiality which the defeat of evil sets up. The overall effect of this poem is comic, since nothing potentially tragic (for example, the storm) prevails.[11] By mode is meant the authorial attitude toward the subject matter of the literary work or basically what is expected as a reader reaction. Comic mode implies futural significance, some form of joy at least, life and continuance, interest in the central character in the future, defeat or nullification of negative forces (even to the point of averting tragic occurrences). I have, surely, just defined the effect of *Paradise Regain'd* as Jesus returns to his mother's house, soon to embark on his ministry in the world and do his father's bidding. For Milton this must have been the essence of the comic in life.

10. Cullen, *The Infernal Triad*, p. 125. Cullen's remarks on the following pages and throughout the book wisely emphasize how the two poems are alike, for "companion poems" implies not only complementarity, which I and other writers have stressed, but similarity, which will heighten, and is indeed necessary to heighten, the contrastive and thus complementary nature of two works.

11. Stuart Curran makes the important point that "It is not, then, Milton's focus on mental rather than physical action, not the lack of heroics, not the diminution of the meaning of history that mark the extent of his epic vision: it is rather the exclusion of death from the world of his epic. . . . *Paradise Regained* celebrates the simple, absolute value of life" ("*Paradise Regained*: Implications of Epic,") in Ide and Wittreich, *Composite Orders*, p. 220.

No one has doubted the tragic mode of *Samson Agonistes*, regardless of the specific definition employed (although questions have been raised about its being a tragedy). Only the somewhat comic figure of Harapha or his lines, the Chorus's overblown description of Dalila, and some of the poetry (largely the obstreperous rhyme) of a few choruses have raised a question of dismay alongside recognition of "the Poets error of intermixing Comic stuff with Tragic sadness and gravity," as Milton remarks in the prefatory "Of the Dramatick Poem," written for publication around 1670. Futural significance is not important for the reader of *Samson*, since the reader is concerned only with Samson, now dead, not with Manoa, Dalila, Harapha, or even the people of Dan, despite the irony of their continued subservence. There can be no joy, even if some of the antagonists have received retribution; the negative forces are not nullified. Nor are we involved in life and continuance. The tragic *Samson Agonistes* which arises against the comic *Paradise Regain'd*, with greater focus because of their order, darkens whatever catharsis is felt and underlines the waste that has been endured in achieving a triumph of will over weakness. Here, as against the comic of the companion poem, is the essence of the tragic. Mere capitulation to weakness, transitory or unremitted, is not the core: the waste in finally achieving the "fairer Paradise" which humankind always seems to exact for itself is.

The order of the poems in the volume is logical on two counts: *Paradise Regain'd* links with *Paradise Lost*, directly in its opening sections but also in its development of a major theme of the longer epic; and *Samson Agonistes* moves to the real from the ideal, to the common condition of all men, to the world itself. The reality of the world in *Paradise Lost* is only to begin as Adam and Eve leave Paradise (although we have viewed that world in speculation in books XI and XII): to understand the meaning of the condition of that real world we need to contrast the ideal. The volume does not offer the buoying up that perhaps the reversal of the poems might have created, but Milton's message has never been involved in that kind of falseness, a point to be remembered, I think, as we end

Lycidas. The fresh woods and pastures new are not going to be without the anxieties defined by the gadding vine, the thankless muse, the fatal and perfidious bark, or the blind mouths. *Samson Agonistes* exemplifies the world that one man chose until Providence truly became his guide; *Paradise Regain'd*, by appearing first, has sharpened the reader's understanding of choice and its commitments. Like an early Jonathan Edwards, Milton can be seen to suggest that freedom of will is lessened each time one makes a choice: the Son keeps his freedom of will by choosing not to act; Samson lessens his freedom each time he chooses to act. What men must learn, Milton implies, is that action should maintain a confederacy with God, who will contribute to that action as guide or provider.

I have indicated another important contrast between these two poems in an article on Milton's concept of covenant.[12] In *Paradise Regain'd* the covenant of grace, existent since the protevangelium, is undergoing change into the New Covenant during the time period of the poem. Milton believed that the Mosaic Law as delivered on Mount Sinai was part of the covenant of grace, not a covenant of works, and that the New Covenant, "MUCH MORE EXCELLENT AND PERFECT THAN THE LAW" (Yale Prose, VI.521), abolished the Old Covenant. As I comment, "the tension of the poem is that between the Old Covenant, which was represented by the Law and which gave promise of Messiah, and the New Covenant which is represented by inward law and which is in the process of being created by the Messiah who has come." Satan knows none of this, although the Son is certainly aware that he himself is the Messiah. Satan's temptations, thus, try to get the Son to abrogate the Law and thereby, whether man or man/god, fall from grace. But the Son is filled with an inward law which is asserted and reasserted as its maintenance becomes increasingly difficult.[13] In contrast is *Samson Agonistes* in which the

12. See Shawcross "Milton and Covenant," *Milton and Scriptural Tradition*, pp. 160–91.
13. Compare James Egan's study, *The Inward Teacher: Milton's Rhetoric of Christian Liberty* (University Park: Pennsylvania State University, 1980), which, dealing with the prose, concludes that Milton "records for posterity eternal Christian truths which are ends in themselves and valid . . . [though] kept alive by the lonely witness of a solitary individual" (p. 90).

central character can operate only under the Law in his
maintenance of the covenant of grace. He, as Hebraic hero,
conceives of works as his action in asserting covenant—the
slaying of the men at Ashkelon, the hundred foxes, the ass's
jawbone. He has, in Milton's view, been wrong, for real
achievement comes through action of the inward spirit. It is
through the temptations of Manoa, Dalila, and Harapha that
Samson is able to develop inward law as he retreats from
engagement with mere "works" or rejects them. Succumbing
to the first temptation offered by Manoa would constitute
relief from Mosaic law, which under the covenant of grace
would be an abrogation of the covenant by Samson.[14] Such
relief denied, Samson has begun a process of renovation,[15]
that which all men can undergo, for God "excludes no man
from the way of penitence and eternal salvation, unless that
man has continued to reject and despise the offer of grace, and
of grace sufficient for salvation, until it is too late" (Yale
Prose, VI.194).

While the Son has inward law and exhibits it under in-
creasingly distressful circumstances, Samson develops such
inward law (his "inward eyes" are illuminated) and proceeds
to his one great work of deliverance, not constrained, not
knowing what cause draws him, knowing only that he is now
able to do something but "Nothing dishonourable, impure,
unworthy/Our God, our Law, my Nation, or my self" (*SA*
1424–25). The deliverance is a self-deliverance and in that is
a model for the deliverance of each person of the tribe of Dan
from the hands of the Philistines. But they do not understand
such inwardness: the great deliverer was to operate externally
of them and thereby bring independence. *Samson Agonistes* thus
complements *Paradise Regain'd*, where the New Covenant is
developed through the Son's actions and contrasted with the
Old Covenant under which Satan operates, by exemplifying

14. The same point is to be seen in Milton's use of *sit* and *stand*; see my discussion
in "A Metaphoric Approach to Reading Milton," *Ball State University Forum* 8 (1967):
17–22.
15. It is by "MAN'S RENOVATION that he is BROUGHT TO A STATE OF
GRACE AFTER BEING CURSED AND SUBJECTED TO GOD'S ANGER"
(Yale Prose, VI.453).

the concept of a covenant of works. Read as a dramatic poem
(rather than as a play), one of the major questions of interpre-
tation of *Samson Agonistes* may be solved: its dramatic propor-
tion suggests an organic developing pattern, and its poetic
proportion emphasizes the internalization which is available
to the reader as the inward law emerges from within Samson.

The renovation of Samson (his turning back to God) is
developed by confirmation of the self and the past (as in the
prologos, *parados*, and first episode), by conquering the assaults
that have triumphed in the past (as in the three central
episodes of ease, worldly position, and pride), and by action
(as developed in the fifth episode and reported in the *exodos*).
The example of the Son (his dedication to God) is observed by
his confirmation of self and the uncertain future (in his solilo-
quy of Book I), by rejection of self-concerns (in the first
temptation), by confuting the worldly goods of wealth, power,
glory (in the second temptation), and by faith (in the third
temptation). Thus we have rejection, confutation, and faith all
equating action of the inward spirit. It should be clear that the
"movement" of the middle episodes of *Samson Agonistes*, though
these offer dialogue, presents types in Manoa, Dalila, and
Harapha who beset Samson's inward being almost as if in a
dream vision, not in a truly real action, only in a verisimilar
one. Samson is exercised as a stalwart, unmoving central
character (not unlike the Son in this regard) assailed by
externalities that do not penetrate to cause relapse. Each
situation seems to penetrate more than the one preceding,
however, almost to reach the point just short of relapse
through anger. Because of the dramatic form of *Samson Agonis-
tes*, expecting representations of reality as in a play, we have
missed the typological dimensions of Manoa, Dalila, and
Harapha, as well as their metaphoric stances. They represent
as surely as Belial, Mammon, and Moloch do in the Infernal
Council in Book II of *Paradise Lost* the lures of ease, wealth,
and pride, being types and metaphors, not truly father, wife,
and enemy.

Problems in interpretation and understanding that have
apparently existed in terms of the 1671 volume for scholars

may be removed, I think, by recognizing the complementarity of the works: together they form a whole for man, depicting life in all its bifurcations, and thus a whole which is both sequel and companion to *Paradise Lost*. Typical, perhaps, of misinterpretation which has fostered a supposed problem is Parker's comment on what he considered "the substance and language of [*Paradise Regain'd*'s] gratuitous comment on both women and Greek tragedy." Parker wrote, "To move, in the 1671 volume from Book IV of *Paradise Regained* on to the Preface of *Samson Agonistes* is to encounter intellectual confusion."[16] It would seem the works were quite separate in thought for him, *Samson* being earlier, *Paradise Regain'd* at a distance in time and thus encompassing later concepts. There is no intellectual confusion on Milton's part between the poems, whatever their dates. The Preface to *Samson Agonistes*, however, may be for the reader literarily disruptive, lying between the two poems as it does. But that preface should be chalked up to Milton's reaction to the contemporary theatrical context—and so perhaps it includes the pointed disavowal of its stage intention—which in 1669–70 had seen produced and printed John Dryden's *Conquest of Granada* and *Tyrannic Love* with such absurdities that George Villiers, Duke of Buckingham's satiric *The Rehearsal* enjoyed repute in the same year that Milton's volume appeared.

The so-called gratuitous comment on women is not a comment on "women" at all but on the supplying of numerous women for sexual purposes only, as Belial implies. Milton is not casting any aspersion on moral sexual experience or woman or women. Satan rejects Belial's lure (the "fond desire" of II.211) for Jesus, for he understands Jesus as a moral being. He rejects "the bait of Women" (II.204) and dotage "on womankind, admiring/Thir shape, thir colour, and attractive grace" (II.175–76). He does not reject marital relationship for Jesus, nor can he, despite the rather obtusely prudish reactions of some readers who really seem incapable of reading with understanding Milton's classification of the

16. Parker, *Milton: A Biography*, vol. 2, p. 1139.

previous items as "toys" (II.177), which "Fall flat and shrink into a trivial toy" (II.223) once admiration is gone. Milton's is a strongly antisexist view. The passage provides a clever way by which Milton was able to include sexual temptation for the Son of God, as we have remarked, without actually including it. He had to make some reference to sexual appetite, for it is such a major influence in man's life (and the Son had emptied himself of godhead!), aside from its obvious relationship with the lure of *voluptaria* in the full-scale temptation motif. Milton is putting down promiscuous sex, not sex, and certainly not marital sex. In the Son we have the sexually abstemious; in contrast Samson is able to unite the temptation of sex and marital sex by convincing himself that the woman of Timna and then Dalila are both worthy to be his wife, only to find himself wrong. But he should have known, of course, that their harlotry might involve sexual insincerity. It is clear that he had been led by his sexual appetite and has rationalized his position to make himself (as agent for his God) psychologically acceptable to himself. The comment in *Paradise Regain'd* is neither pertinent to the point Parker was alleging nor gratuitous: it stresses a motif that is contrasted in *Samson Agonistes*. If we cannot read *Paradise Regain'd* adequately, we have the more human *Samson Agonistes* to help us. The complementarity of the two poems is evident in even this relatively small point of substance and thought.

The alleged rejection of Greek learning in *Paradise Regain'd* on Milton's part has had a long history of explication, most of it out of context of the temptation motif of which it is a part. This section is part of the second temptation to worldly things and covetousness; it does not involve seeming necessity but plurality and nonessentiality. The second temptation presents lures that impinge on man's relationship with his community, as I have indicated before. The Son argues for basic knowledge and wisdom as against pluralities and nonessential matter (because of their being derived from or being ancillary to the basic knowledge in the Bible and particularly in the Psalms). Community, however, is impressed by fine and numerous images of intellectual show. The comment on the tragedians (IV.261–66), in the midst of the temptation to assert knowledge over one's fellow man, is neither pertinent to what Parker was assigning it (a "later utterance of Milton's spirit") nor gratuitous: the Son rejects Satan's temptation, and in so doing rejects as "plural" and "nonessential" the alleged "doctrine," the "moral prudence," the "sage Philosophy" which the Greek oratory listed subtends. His point is that wisdom lies in the teachings of God as seen in *"Sion's* songs," in the plainness of the prophets, in the rather singular substance of the Bible, which offers essential knowledge. Satan talks of the "lofty grave Tragoedians" who best teach

> moral prudence, with delight receiv'd
> In brief sententious precepts, while they treat
> Of fate, and chance, and change in human life;
> High actions, and high passions best describing.
> (IV.261–66)

But the Son rejects the necessity of an intervener, an interpreter for him "who receives/Light from above, from the fountain of light"; he "no other doctrine needs, *though granted true* [emphasis mine]" (IV.288–90). He neither grants such doctrine true or not true, but he certainly does not reject it as meaningful for some people. The implication is unhidden: there are those who do not receive the light from above which is open to them. The "better teaching" of the prophets is lost on them. For them some intermediary presentation of "moral prudence, with delight" is necessary, and it is for this reason that Spenser was a better teacher than Aquinas, since the "delight" is missing from the latter's work. For humankind Milton's *Paradise Regain'd* and *Samson Agonistes* are needed when there are those who have not received the light from above: Milton, the eternal teacher, offers a direction for those seeking the path to salvation. Its offering through "delight" should be more effective than its offering through only the prudence of, say, *De doctrina christiana*. The question of the alleged rejection of learning has resulted from ill-reading critics who have allowed their own prejudices toward Greek and Roman authors to blind them to what the poem in context records as the Son's words.

The concept of *dulce* in the midst of *utile* is made doubly tangible as we move in the 1671 volume from *Paradise Regain'd* to *Samson Agonistes*, for the reader (people) can identify with this work's central figure, who is human, more easily than with a man/God. Such verisimilitude is a staple of the effect of dramatic form where the distance between stage presentation and audience is foreshortened by identification with the acted roles even though separation by the space of the nondialogic between actor and viewer impedes internalization of any traffic upon that stage. For those who need an intermediary presentation of "moral prudence, with delight," we have a dramatic presentation based on the arts of Greece (indeed, most purposefully *on the arts of Greece*): its substance comes to praise God aright, to reject "Fortune and Fate" in favor of Providence, and to express "moral vertue . . . By light of Nature not in all quite lost" (*PR* IV.251–52). The plainness of *Paradise Regain'd*, the "majestic unaffected stile," is consciously adhered to as contrast with the "swelling Epithetes" of the dramatic Greek form which takes its substance from the "Law and Story" of God's accommodated fountain of light.

We have in these two works published together complementary forces that contrast forms and structures, genres and modes, poetic styles and tone, characters and narrative, treatment of the subject matter, the forms of heroic action, the suprahuman and the distressingly human. But also present is the duplication of message, covenantal concerns, the substance of the subject matter, and means "to imbreed and cherish in a great people the seeds of vertu" (*Reason of Church-Government*, Yale Prose, I.816). *Paradise Lost* had failed, or so it seemed: witness its apparent lack of significance between 1667 and 1669, when six successive issues were deemed necessary, and its lack of general reputation until the fourth edition of 1688; witness that question Ellwood had put to Milton at Chalfont St. Giles. Both works—the diffuse epic and the 1671 volume—were needed in order for Milton to achieve "thos intentions which [had] liv'd within [him] ever since [he] could conceiv [himself] any thing worth to [his] Countrie" (*Reason of Church-Government*, Yale Prose, I.820). *Paradise Regain'd* offered truth to the intellect; *Samson Agonistes*, to the heart. Wisdom cries out from all places, both the tops thereof and in the streets.

Chapter Nine

The Political Dimension

I T has been a commonplace that *Paradise Regain'd* is not a political poem—despite a chapter in *Heroic Knowledge* in which Arnold Stein presented "A Digression on Poetry and Politics." Perhaps an underlying factor has been a comparison with *Paradise Lost*, which has so frequently been interpreted for political theory, or in terms of Milton's beliefs as demonstrated in various works, or as reflection of contemporary events. But Milton's "other" poem should also be examined in terms of Milton's beliefs, not only by application of beliefs discovered in other works but by recognition of a political dimension in the undercurrents of *Paradise Regain'd* itself and its message. While there are matters to bring to bear on the poem as far as political theory is concerned and as far as political contexts may impinge, it is really the Miltonic cast of thought that removes this poem from delimitations of "religion" and "politics" and moves the reader into recognition of its lasting contribution.

Milton, alongside Thomas Hobbes or John Locke, has been relegated to unimportance by constitutional historians. It may be hard for students of Milton to admit, but he was not some kind of cog in the machinery of Commonwealth government or a direct force in the issues of the time or their settlements. Subtly he may have had effect on foreign traffic with the English government by his state correspondence and his association with foreign diplomats. But we should remember that Sir Bulstrode Whitelocke referred to him as "one Mr. *Milton*, a blind man"[1] and that he nowhere enters the Earl of Clarendon's *History of the Rebellion and Civil Wars*. Such narratives of the course of history during the Interregnum, however, are concerned with the overt, and constitutional historians are concerned with direct and tangible action. Ultimately Milton was a significant political thinker through the influence of his ideas working more subtly, as George Sensabaugh has shown: "He in fact contributed so vigorously to the victory of principles which lay at the basis of the Revolutionary Settlement and the Bill of Rights that long before Whigs of the eighteenth century made him an oracle of political wisdom Tories had already with accuracy, if with considerable irony, deemed him 'that grand whig *Milton*.' "[2]

Still, much of that influence stayed within the generally practical and legalistic. Even more significant, I think, is the philosophic substruct which leads to practical and legal acts. As Christopher Hill expressed it, Milton's "fluid conception of Christ's kingdom" in *Paradise Regain'd* "was not an Utopian model constitution: it was rather a state of mind, not fixed once for all."[3] The philosophic substruct we find iterated from *The Tenure of Kings and Magistrates* by Algernon Sidney as he was about to be hanged for treason is the important one for the 150 years following Milton's death: "That God had left Nations unto the Liberty of settling up such Governments as best pleased themselves./That Magistrates were set up for the good of Nations, not Nations for the honour or glory of Magistrates./That the Right and Power of Magistrates in every Country, was that which the Laws of that Country made it to be./That those Laws were to be observed, and the Oaths taken by them, having the force of a Contract between Magistrate and People, could not be Violated without danger

1. Sir Bulstrode Whitelocke, *Memorials of the English Affairs* (London, 1682), p. 633.

2. George Sensabaugh, *That Grand Whig, Milton* (Palo Alto: Stanford University Press, 1952; New York: Benjamin Blom, 1967), p. 4.

3. Christopher Hill, *Milton and the English Revolution* (New York: Viking Press, 1977), p. 416.

of dissolving the whole Fabrick."[4] I have previously argued from a study of *Tenure* that Milton does make a contribution to political theory, although it is to be derived from his discussion rather than from its being laid out as a philosophic treatise. The idealistic Milton believed that "Only by *preventing* evil from existing within each person . . . could a full state of freedom be attained, and the most oppressive of internal forces is self-pride. . . . For freedom cannot be freedom unless it exists for everyone, and it cannot 'exist' for more than a few if thought and action are not disciplined to foster freedom for everyone equally at all times."[5] Milton's is the opposite of Hobbes's belief: one re-forms the people, not sets up institutions "to keep them in the way."[6] Reformation of institutions will achieve nothing for long. He sought for humankind "the experience of a world that is not to be mastered and controlled but to be liberated"[7] by a proper regard for self in every person and by a proper regard of each person for every other person. That the substance of *Paradise Regain'd* expresses these thoughts, once distance from a biblist view of the poem is reached, has been the burden of the preceding chapters of this volume.

The "message" of the poem results from the honest view of self which we have talked about as the nub of the first temptation: when one has conquered self, the world of evil can have no internal effect. Though it externally immanacle the body (as the earlier statement of the concept in *A Maske* acknowledged), evil cannot immanacle the inner being. And if all had such inner being, "speckl'd vanity/[Would] sicken soon and die,/And leprous sin [would] melt from earthly

4. *A Very Copy of a Paper Delivered to the Sheriffs, Upon the Scaffold on Tower-Hill, on Friday, Decemb. 7. 1683* (London, 1683), p. 2.

5. John T. Shawcross, "The Higher Wisdom of *The Tenure of Kings and Magistrates*," in *Achievements of the Left Hand: Essays on the Prose of John Milton*, ed. Michael Lieb and John T. Shawcross (Amherst: University of Massachusetts Press, 1974), p. 154.

6. Thomas Hobbes, *Leviathan*, ed. Michael Oakeshott (Oxford: Basil Blackwell, 1960), pt. 2, ch. 30, p. 227.

7. The words are Herbert Marcuse's in *Eros and Civilization* (Boston: Beacon Press, 1966), p. 164.

mould" ("On the Morning of Christs Nativity," 136–38).
"Milton's political theory is based on his moral theory, on the
individual state of man," Stein wrote. "The ideal state is a
union of ideal individuals, and what is true for the single state
of man is true, by extension, for the multiple state of the
nation. . . . The real political arena is the self, where duty
must be understood and managed. Self-mastery achieved by
obedience to truth is the best preparation for executing the
commands of truth. . . ."[8] As we range over Milton's various
prose works, despite their being directly tied in most cases to
specific current debates and specific books which he aimed to
confute, we can truly comprehend certain statements only
through our articulation of his broad moral/political position.
When he proclaims that "true and substantial liberty . . .
must be sought, not without, but within, and . . . is best
achieved, not by the sword, but by a life rightly undertaken
and rightly conducted,"[9] we should be bringing into mind the
message we have discerned in the brief epic. When he
counsels, "learn to obey right reason, to master yourselves"
(p. 684), we know that he is urging not only the exemplar of
the Son as Man upon us—not really the exemplary at all, as I
have previously remarked—but how to live one's life, with
achievement of independence from others through indepen-
dence from the lures of self. The rite of passage from depen-
dence whether from parents, relatives, friends, or even from
one's god to independence is the only means to "refrain from
factions, hatreds, superstitions, injuries, lusts, and rapine
against one another" (p. 684).

The sad dependence of humankind upon God to save them
I have discussed previously in looking at the tragedy of hope
in the companion poem *Samson Agonistes*.[10] Here is another
point in the wisdom of their dual publication: while *Paradise
Regain'd* sets forth the need for and means to independence of
the individual, *Samson Agonistes* existentially lays bare the lack
of individuality in the group mind when anxiety and fear and

8. Stein, *Heroic Knowledge*, p. 65.
9. *Defensio secunda*, Yale Prose, IV, i (1966), 624, trans. Helen North.
10. See "Irony as Tragic Effect" in Wittreich, *Calm of Mind*.

ease, particularly ease, cloud it. It is so much easier not to act
and to arrogate action to others, particularly to God. The
poems together underscore Milton's message dialectically:
Satan offers to deliver up to the Son what he is reputedly
destined for, kingdom; and the Danites await a Great De-
liverer to achieve their kingdom and abolish their slavery.[11]
The act of the unassisted but faith-filled Son defines the act
that Samson must accomplish, and it is only through such act,
Milton asserts over and over, that humankind in its political
world can be victorious. The selflessness of the Son must
prevail over the personal works of aggrandizement shown by
the Samson of the past: the standard of rule, Milton learned
from Aristotle and Erasmus, is not the private; it is the
common interest of all people. And yet another way to look at
Samson Agonistes, though we verge on the allegoric, is to under-
stand that the way to true peace and ease and "the blissful
Seat" is to act in this world, certainly not simply await and
certainly not simply lead the cloistered life.

In his "practical" solution for the restraint of monarchic
rule, undoubtedly to return within a few months in 1660,
Milton proposed a perpetual senate which would be the basis
for a "free Commonwealth." "And why should we thus dis-
parage and prejudice our own nation, to govern us," he
argued, "if we will but use diligence and impartiality to finde
them out and chuse them, rather yoking our selves to a single
person, the natural adversarie and oppressor of libertie,
though good, yet far easier corruptible by the excess of his
singular power and exaltation, or at best, not comparably
sufficient to bear the weight of government, nor equally dis-
pos'd to make us happie in the enjoyment of our libertie under
him."[12] In light of the moral/political position that has
emerged from our reading of *Paradise Regain'd* and other works,

11. Even were a Great Deliverer able to free the subjugated Danites from the
Philistines (and one may substitute for these names any noun denominating any
group or any abstraction), Milton foresaw that "Peace itself will be by far [their]
hardest war, and what [they] thought liberty will prove to be [their] servitude"
unless there be true and sincere devotion to God and men (*Defensio secunda*, p. 680).

12. Robert W. Ayers, ed., *The Readie and Easie Way to Establish a Free Commonwealth*,
2d ed., Yale Prose, VII, rev. ed., p. 449.

the statement has some important curiosities, after one has discounted the effects of purposeful argument toward a contemporary circumstance. This reinstalled king becomes "the natural adversarie and oppressor of libertie" by dint of being "single." The single person is more easily attacked, more easily corrupted: we think of Eve leaving Adam to garden separately, or we think of the man Jesus alone in a wilderness. Both are "good, yet far easier corruptible," and through fraud one of these falls though the other remain inviolate. The garden whether that of the Edenic world or that metaphor which images the world of England at peace becomes a context in which one's guard is down. And though it is through the individual and then through many individuals together that salvation for the person and for the group can come, this passage from *The Ready and Easy Way* plays upon the inherent problems of singularity, in the same reversed way that Milton is playing upon "ready" and "easy," neither of which depicts his approach to the resolution of moral issues. The transfer of "adversary" (remembering the word *Satan* etymologically) to the single person as one thus "naturally" opposed to the group, making the group here the people of England as a whole, subtly renders the governmental issue ontological. The "able and worthie men" who may keep any individual king in check presents a thought which rests upon the concept that all men are subject to the adversary but that they are subject to the adversary less when they complement one another to fill in whatever may be a chink in an individual's moral armor. Every one of these "able and worthie men" may not each by himself approach the ideal which the Son as Man presents, but together they may form a group that will get nearer.

A similar concern of the difficulties of the single unit against the adversary or the more potential success of the united effort of many single entities against a common enemy pervades Milton's last tract, *Of True Religion, Hæresie, Schism, Toleration* (1673): "And if all Protestants as universally as they hold these two Principles, so attentively and Religiously would observe them, they would avoid and cut off many Debates and

Contentions, Schisms and Persecutions, which too oft have been among them, and more firmly unite against the common adversary" and "But if they who dissent in matters not essential to belief, while the common adversary is in the field, shall stand jarring and pelting at one another, they will be soon routed and subdued."[13] Here the common adversary is the Papacy, the Roman Catholic Church. But each single unit should be forged into the resistant entity that will not succumb to the wiles of the Papacy: "The last means to avoid Popery, is to amend our lives" (p. 438). The more private and singular is thus seen as the base out of which the command and composite interest can have effect. The "excessively vitious" nature of "this Nation of late years" has given itself over to the lures of the second temptation, "Luxury, Drunkenness, Whoredom," and the third, "Pride, . . . Cursing, Swearing, bold and open Atheism." The greatest peril, however, more potential because our lives need amending, is the superstition of Romish doctrine: "easy Confession, easy Absolution, Pardons, Indulgences, Masses for him both quick and dead, *Agnus Dei's*, Reliques, and the like" (p. 439). The two principles indicated above are: ". . . the Rule of true Religion is the Word of God only: and . . . their Faith ought not to be an implicit faith, that is, to believe . . . against or without express authority of Scripture" (p. 420). We might compare this with the Son's admonishment to Satan, "do as thou find'st/Permission from above; thou canst not more" (I.495–96), and his conviction that "he who receives/Light from above, from the fountain of light,/No other doctrine needs, though granted true" (IV.288–90). The so-called rejection of learning which follows, the doctrines being false, dreams, conjectures, fancies, is not dissimilar to the rejection of religious "Debates and Contentions, Schisms and Persecutions." Milton does not so much reject sectarianism as he argues that true religion has a fundament deriving from the Word of God, seen in and interpretable from the Scriptures. The pervasive root is faith in that Word of God and thus in the God who spoke it.

13. Yale Prose, VIII, 420 and 436.

An important statement when read against what we have been discussing as the message of *Paradise Regain'd* and its political application is Sonnet 15, addressed to Sir Thomas Fairfax and written in August 1648, on the occasion of his capture of Colchester, which became the finishing event of the second Civil War. The need at times for war and military aggressiveness is not denied, but "a nobler task" must ensue, for wars will breed only endless war. That nobler task to which Fairfax is urged—well before the parliamentary action of apprehending, trying, and executing the king—is to free Truth and Right from Violence, to replace Public Fraud by Public Faith and thereby disengage faith from fraud. The Avarice of the lure of the second temptation and the Rapine of the third, which would seem to ravage England, make Valour bleed in vain. Milton is no way even considering regicide as a path of action, and of course in *The Tenure of Kings and Magistrates* he does not argue *for* it, only that such strong action may on occasion be necessary. (The tract was being written while the trial was taking place, and rumors were rife about its outcome and the possibility of execution.) Fairfax is exhorted to step in in 1648 and become a great deliverer: full deliverance will not just happen, nor will it be accomplished by one whose virtue seems shakable by vanity or praise. Fairfax must have struck Milton in mid-1648 as one whose personal integrity had conquered self and seen through the fraudulent, including such fraudulence as the Scots' leaguing with truth for their own advantage. Milton's estimate of Fairfax was, of course, reinforced and borne out when he resigned his governmental association in June 1650 and retired to his estate in Yorkshire because of the intended (and in July dispatched) invasion of Scotland unprovoked by any specific military act of aggression against the English.[14] Of

14. Milton also praises Fairfax in *Defensio secunda*; see Yale Prose, IV, i, 669–70. The editor of this tract, Donald A. Roberts, believed Milton's admiration was sincere but exaggerated, apparently because Fairfax did not concern himself with public affairs as the sonnet was urging upon him. Roberts's reading of the sonnet is not mine: he says, "it expresses also the belief that Fairfax was destined to be a notable statesman." Of course, it says nothing of the kind. See note 497, p. 669.

course, Milton must have been chagrined that Fairfax did not rise to a position to exact that nobler task. Perhaps in 1648 Milton would not have commended Oliver Cromwell, although he was clearly a major leader of what would be a new political alignment, because of suspicions that he less approached the ideal of selflessness than Milton believed was always necessary. In *Defensio secunda* Milton remarks, "he was a soldier well-versed in self-knowledge, and whatever enemy lay within—vain hopes, fears, desires—he had either previously destroyed within himself or had long since reduced to subjection. Commander first over himself, victor over himself, he had learned to achieve over himself the most effective triumph . . ."[15]—which has a decided hint of uncertainty about it still. The well-known sonnet addressed to Cromwell deepens that hint.

Sonnet 16, written in May 1652 as an ostensible plea for liberty of conscience and against remuneration of the clergy (which would make the clergy hirelings, in Milton's way of thinking, and their gospel dependent upon the government that supported them), has two curiously ambiguous lines in this context: "Guided by faith and matchless Fortitude/To peace and truth thy glorious way has plough'd." While everything seems positive, commendatory, that word *plough'd* has connotations and encases an allusion that give one pause. The ploughing suggests the humble figure of Piers,[16] who had offered to guide pilgrims to Truth, but Cromwell has ploughed his way with glory by military victories. The theological sections of *Piers the Plowman* on reason, conscience, and the clergy which predicate the corruption of the Church and the merit of poverty seem particularly apt for this sonnet on

15. Ibid., pp. 667–68. Roberts's note (p. 668 n. 492) is: "For eight years, from 1628 to 1636, he wrestled with God and, beset by awful doubts and terrible fears, he resisted that service which he knew was perfect freedom." This was a period when Cromwell was sometimes in parliament, a tradesman, Lord of the Fens, in financial difficulties, somewhat on the fringes of Puritanism. Milton may refer to "unconfirmed stories of extravagance and mismanagement in his early days, of the sort that tend to gather round men who are later to be famous" (Christopher Hill, *God's Englishman: Oliver Cromwell and the English Revolution* [New York: Harper & Row, 1972], p. 45).

16. At least one very explicit reference to William Langland's poem exists; see *An Apology Against a Pamphlet*, Yale Prose, I.916.

hireling ministers. It is a subtle reminder to Cromwell that the proposed function of the Committee for the Propagation of the Gospel will "bind our souls with secular chains." But further, there is an allusion here to Luke 9:62: "And Jesus said unto him, No man, having put his hand to the plow, and looking back, is fit for the kingdom of God." It is indeed a veiled threat that Cromwell, now having achieved at least some sense of truth and the perilous path to it, must proceed onward to other victories than only the military ones. After all, he has plowed his way to peace as well, and further militarism is hardly the praiseworthy outcome of peace. It is the same kind of exhortation that is the focus of the Fairfax sonnet. Cromwell should neither look back on his victories, nor continue in the same way: "Valour should not bleed in vain." Any man, having put his hand to the plow, and moving on in his faithful work, is fit for the kingdom of God.

Both sonnets, to Fairfax and to Cromwell, make appeals to men in position to act for the good of the people. They are implored to act, and to act in a way that is selfless. The Son's thoughts in his first soliloquy, already referred to in chapter 6, reprise his formerly envisioned heroic acts and victorious deeds, the subduing and quelling of violence and tyranny; *then persuasion of the stubborn with words*. More remains than only military victory. But of course Fairfax will disappoint: he chooses exile to action; he avoids any sustained confrontation. Cromwell on the other hand does sally forth, and though Milton may have had some of his suspicions about Cromwell confirmed by the Instrument of the Protectorate, he wisely knew that some action was needed in 1653 when, in 1654, he finally was able to recover from personal loss and incapacity to get back into the fray, trying to persuade some of the stubborn and ill-informed by his new words. Still one wonders whether the governmental actions of 1653, conservative as they were and killing of radical ideas, did not join the personal disasters to cause a kind of exile for Milton himself.[17] Hill

17. Of his own work we know only nine state papers dated (or probably dated) in 1653—eight are given under this date by J. Max Patrick in the Yale Prose, V, ii (1971), but there is also the Safeguard for the Duke of Holstein—and a personal letter to John Bradshaw.

remarks of this period, "The Fifth Monarchist Vavasor Pow-
ell greeted the Protectorate by asking his congregation
whether the Lord would have 'Oliver Cromwell, or Jesus
Christ to reign over us.' A few months earlier the two had not
seemed to be rivals."[18]

Although she is writing about *Samson Agonistes*, a comment
by Mary Ann Radzinowicz is as pertinent to *Paradise Regain'd*
and iterates in part some of the views developed in earlier
discussions of this book: "Milton accepted that the law of God
is the force of individual liberty given to men to fulfill them-
selves both as private and social beings, to band themselves
together against all who opposed that law of liberty, and to
become God's chosen people. The law of nations and the law
of nature are both derived from the free following of the spirit
of truth and reason in the individual."[19] *Paradise Regain'd* is
devoted to establishing the means to that individual liberty;
its political dimension lies in its need and employment in
public service. It is that public service that is overwhelmingly
manifest: it is the ministry of Jesus after he has returned home
to his mother's house; it is the duty of charity toward our
neighbor; it is the political duties of the magistrate and the
people either to the other, which Milton defines in *De doctrina
christiana*, Book II, Chapter XVII. But it is not simply attrib-
utable to one's birth: for Milton it was a moral characteristic,
engendered by such virtues as honesty (particularly to the
self) and godliness (particularly the prevenient grace which a
person has accepted from God). These concepts can be
found throughout Milton's writing, whether poetry or prose,
whether early or late. He does move from institutionalism,
such as the church as administrative unit, and he does in-
creasingly emphasize the individual, but political institution
cannot be voided, for here, unlike religious life, an organiza-
tion is necessary to allow the individual to function with other
individuals without infractions from those who oppose that
law of liberty, whether by precept or by deed. Hobbes's belief
that "hedges" will "keep them in the way" looks at the

18. Hill, *God's Englishman*, p. 145.
19. Radzinowicz, *Toward Samson Agonistes*, p. 169.

situation in the opposite direction from Milton. What is striking about Satan's omission of the phrase "to keep thee in all thy ways" from Psalm 91 during the third temptation is that same kind of negative and fatalistic thinking that the ways of the faithful servant of God can only be driven by self. Hobbes wants the "hedges" so that people cannot exercise their free choice, for their free choice would bring injustice and chaos. The psalm says that God will aid humankind when something occurs that may bring harm as the people follow their free choice of their "ways," which ways, however, are the courses of action that God's chosen people, as godly people, will take. Satan's omission of the phrase offers up the false solace exemplified by the Danites of the Samson story that God will aid his sons regardless of their actions, while at the same time he collapses the plural sense to a specific, individual person and occasion, appropriate to the pride being tested. The political organization, or the "hedges," will, in Milton's thinking, allow humankind to keep in their ways by creating a force that will counter the opposition to their keeping in their ways. The greatest force to oppose one's keeping in his way is the force of Satan, whose influence lies through the self, through inordinate desire, and through vanity, the subjects of the three temptations. Fortified against such temptation, men can band together to maintain the law of liberty which has fortified them. The start for such idealistic life on earth (and Jesus does *not* refute the possibility of an earthly nation under God and does *not* set up the rationalizations of an afterlife I mentioned at the beginning of chapter 6) is the proper regard for self in every person and the proper regard of each person for every other person—the intrinsic message of *Paradise Regain'd*.

The thrust of an essay by Jackie Di Salvo on *Samson Agonistes* is that Milton's dramatic poem parallels what was occurring with and within the Puritan revolution. Samson "is fighting on God's side in a cosmic war against Satan, whose battlefield is not only in the soul but in the political terrain of England. . . . The contrast between Samson and Harapha reflects the development of a new kind of soldier armed with the advantages of internal discipline."[20] She demonstrates the currency for the 1640s and 1650s of Samson as military hero against political enslavement. As complementary poem, *Paradise Regain'd* reflects the same kind of cosmic war against Satan but in a more philosophic, rather than experiential, realm, and it develops that internal discipline necessary for the war of the saints against adversarial force on a broad and nonparticularized basis. It is Milton's answer to the kind of question that Jung raised about "the power of the creator with respect to the powerless creature" (p. 56): the creature can take on an aspect of the power of the creator by exercise of the godliness within him, as ever in his great taskmaster's eye. The creature need not be essentially powerless.

The substance of the brief epic is found throughout Milton's thought and oeuvre, as I have said, but the need to articulate it clearly and unavoidably in a work that could perform as a better teacher than Aquinas was driven home to Milton by Ellwood's question put to him about "Paradise found." That the appearance of the poem also reflects a commentary upon current world political events as Milton readied his poem for publication is evident, even though Milton probably did not think of them in such juxtaposition. The machinations of political forces during 1667–69 can be seen in the War of Devolution, the deposition of Alfonso VI of Portugal, followed on 13 February 1668, by Spain's recognition of Portugal's independence, the French capture of the Spanish Netherlands, the abdication of John Casmir of Poland on 19 September 1668, and the Turkish conquest of Crete in 1669 after the Venetians had abandoned Candia. More significant still were the movement of the Dutch fleet into the Thames and Medway on 11–13 June 1667, and the ensuing attack on Clarendon House on the fourteenth by a mob openly denouncing Clarendon's treason, although he was not deposed until 30 August and did not flee England until 29 November. Peace with the Dutch came at Breda on 21 July, but the end of the War of Devolution did not officially take place until 2 May 1668, with

20. Jackie Di Salvo, "'The Lord's Battels': *Samson Agonistes* and the Puritan Revolution," *Milton Studies* 4 (1972): 39.

the Treaty of Aix-la-Chapelle, after promulgation of the Triple Alliance of England and Holland (23 January) and Sweden (April) against France. (Louis XIV made peace with Spain on 15 April with the Treaty of St. Germaine, and England's treaty with France had to wait until 21 December 1670, after the secret negotiations at Dover, 22 May–1 June.) At least *we* can hear echoes of current political dilemmas in Satan's:

> how could'st thou hope
> Long to enjoy it quiet and secure,
> Between two such enclosing enemies
> *Roman* and *Parthian*? . . . the *Parthian* first
> By my advice, as nearer and of late
> Found able by invasion to annoy
> Thy country . . .
> Chuse which thou wilt by conquest or by league.
> By him thou shalt regain . . .   (III,359–71)

The Son's answer might be Milton's: "think not thou to find me . . . to need . . . that cumbersome/Luggage of war there shewn me, argument/Of human weakness rather than of strength" (III.398–402).

But if the poem was first envisioned and partially written in the 1640s, even a greater philosophical interaction can be discerned. For the years of 1643–45 saw not only Civil War and the intellectual battle that Di Salvo details but the antagonistic attitudes of those who cried "liberty" but wanted only "license." The audience for *The Tenure of Kings and Magistrates* but a few years later, as the period of retirement from public debate ended, were "those who align themselves with reforms yet draw back as consequent acts, dictated by reason, arise."[21] Man is always victim of himself, but while Stein is partially correct in saying that "Milton's most tangible

21. Shawcross, "The Higher Wisdom," p. 144ff.

suggestions are directed toward negative actions" (p. 66), Milton is also determined that confrontation will yield positive action and that one part of confrontation is uncovering falsity and advancing truth. In *Tenure* Milton tried to persuade the antimonarchic group to support further action through exposing false arguments and emotional tugs upon them over the status of kingship. Thus he hoped to demonstrate that further acts (deposition, even execution) "after due conviction" are not only lawful but incumbent. The argument of *Paradise Regain'd* is a preliminary to such conclusion: the rudiments of the Son's great warfare, Humiliation and strong Sufferance, are supervened by vanquishment of hellish wiles by wisdom and by steadfastness without fear and with resolve. The act of standing is made by choice regardless of the consequences, and once the positive decision to stand is made, there is no turning back. These, Milton perceived, are the "deeds/Above Heroic . . ./Worthy t'have not remain'd so long unsung" (I. 14–17).

Chapter Ten

Afterword

THE questions and the attitudes which *Paradise Regain'd* has raised in critical circles are not going to change. Critics are still going to pay it less attention than they are *Paradise Lost*, place it within an inferior evaluation, look upon it as jejune. Certain critical commentary of the past, whether it has any substantial value or not—like so many ideas that persist in popular minds no matter what the denial of them or the logical invalidating of them—will reemerge to continue to pose "Milton's" "rejection" of "learning," the relationship of the dream in Book II and the storm in Book IV to the temptation motif, the thesis that the Son is trying to learn his identity which provides some kind of suspenseful undercurrent, the nugatory portrait of Satan, the falsity of suggesting that a god figure is anything but constant and perfect. But while the poem has interrelationships with *Paradise Lost* and pursues factors contrastive to *Samson Agonistes* to present its message and view of life, it should be read as an entity unto itself: a literary work that should be understood and evaluated without reader expectation from its contextualization *in the reader's mind* resulting from ideas about others' works or preconceived notions of Milton man, thinker, and poet. One wishes that these critics would read *Milton's* poem, not something of their or another's conceiving.

John Dennis's rejection of the poem because it does not "promote the Violence of the Enthusiastic Passions," and

131

because it is based on "Patience, Resignation, Humility, Meekness, Long-suffering, and the rest of those quiet divine Virtues that adorn the Christian Scheme," elicits the penetrating comment by Dustin Griffin, "For a theorist who aspires to a more perfect sacred poetry, this is a remarkable rejection of the Christian virtues as a foundation for poetry."[1] Dennis's moralistic aesthetic criteria get in the way of valid judgment. Indeed, the comparison of the two epics early brought forth the negative attitude toward *Paradise Regain'd* which is recorded in Bayle's *Dictionary*, "which made some wags say, that Milton is easily found in Paradise Lost but not in Paradice regained."[2] Even Samuel Wesley, a Milton enthusiast, comments, "As for his Paradice Regain'd, I nothing wonder that it has not near the Life of his former Poem, any more than the Odysses fall short of The Iliads. Milton, when he wrote this, was grown older, probably poorer: He had not that scope for Fable, was confin'd to a lower Walk, and draws out that in four Books which might have been well compriz'd in one."[3] The analogy with Homer's works reappears in the next century, strangely enough—as Griffin remarked of Dennis—in his grandson John Wesley's *Journal*, entry for Tuesday, 5 September 1769.[4] Yet Samuel Wesley's poem frequently

1. Dustin Griffin, *Regaining Paradise: Milton and the eighteenth century* (Cambridge: Cambridge University Press, 1986), p. 96. Dennis's remarks are from *The Grounds of Criticism in Poetry* (1704) and *Remarks Upon Several Passages in the Preliminaries to the Dunciad* (1729); see my *Milton: The Critical Heritage* (London: Routledge & Kegan Paul, 1970), pp. 134 and 260. Dennis, talking of "the true use that ought to be made of Religion in Poetry," remarks that "*Milton* indeed happen'd upon it, in his *Paradise Lost*; I say, happen'd upon it, because he err'd very widely from it in his *Paradise Regain'd*" (Dennis, *Grounds of Criticism*, in Shawcross, *Critical Heritage*, p. 134). That word "true" defines the kind of critical stance that epitomizes Dennis's evaluative basis, as well as other post-Restoration critics'.
2. Pierre Bayle, *The Dictionary Historical and Critical*, 2d ed. (1737), in Shawcross, *Critical Heritage*, p. 116. The comment first appeared in John Toland's "Life of John Milton," in *A Complete Collection* (1698), also published separately in 1699.
3. Samuel Wesley, *The Life of Our Blessed Lord and Savior Jesus Christ* (1697), "The Preface, Being an Essay on Heroic Poetry," in Shawcross, *Critical Heritage*, pp. 114–15.
4. See *The Works of Rev. John Wesley, A. M.*, 4th ed. (London: John Mason, 1841), vol. 3, p. 360. He talks of *Paradise Regain'd* as "the last faint effort of an expiring Muse."

imitates and echoes the brief epic, so much so that Nahum
Tate in his commendatory poem "To Mr Samuel Wesley on
his Divine Poem of the Life of Christ" offers the observation
that Wesley's poem "completes" Milton's. The thought that
Paradise Regain'd is not complete was commonplace, directly
and subtly, both in distress over the title, since the poem did
not accomplish the regaining of Paradise, for this would occur
only with the Crucifixion, and in expectation that the Passion
and Crucifixion should have been (possibly may have been
intended as) part of the poem.[5] However, as we would expect,
Thomas Ellwood saw the brief epic in successful conjunction
with the diffuse poem:

Two great Examples of this kind [blank verse] he left
(The natural Issue of his teeming Brain),
Th'one shews how man of Eden was bereft;
In t' other man doth Paradise regain,
So far as naked Nations can attain.[6]

And so did Alexander Oldys, who nonetheless praised John
Dryden's tagging of the long epic in his *The State of Innocence,
and Fall of Man* (1677) and who ranged the poetic achievement
against Milton's political biography, Milton speaking:

"Great bard," said he, "'twas verse alone
Did for my hideous crime atone,
Defending once the worst rebellion . . .

5. Though he does not explicitly raise the specter of incompleteness, Henry John
Todd, as the nineteenth century was beginning, lamented "that the plan is faulty:
For, to attribute the Redemption of Mankind solely to Christ's triumph over the
temptations in the wilderness, is a notion not only contracted, but untrue. The gate of
everlasting life was opened, through the Death and Resurrection of our Lord." (*The
Poetical Works of John Milton* [London, 1801], vol. 5, p. 335.
6. Thomas Ellwood, "Epitaph on Milton" (1675?), in Shawcross, *Critical Heritage*, p. 86.

Thine was indeed the state of innocence,
Mine of offence,
With studied treason and self-interest stained,
Till Paradise Lost wrought Paradise Regained."[7]

The dichotomous opinion of Milton the poet and Milton the
political figure appeared frequently; for example, in Joseph
Addison's "An Account of the Greatest English Poets" (1694)
and Thomas Yalden's "On the Reprinting of Milton's Prose
Works" (1698).[8] The comparison of the two epics continued
to be negative toward *Paradise Regain'd* as in William Warbur-
ton's imperceptive view, "the plan is a very unhappy one, and
defective even in that narrow view of a sequel, for it affords the
poet no opportunity of driving the Devil back again to Hell
from his new conquests in the air,"[9] and infrequently positive
(though not without equivocation) on subjective grounds as in
William Wordsworth's reported opinion of it "as surpassing
even the *Paradise Lost* in execution, though the theme is far
below it and demanding less power."[10] John Jortin confuses
by first saying that "*Milton*'s *Paradise Regain'd* has not met with
the approbation that it deserves," and then immediately
criticizing it in terms of its being lesser than *Paradise Lost* on
four counts. However, somewhat backhandedly, he adds,
"Artful sophistry, false reasoning set off in the most specious

7. Alexander Oldys, *An Ode by Way of Elegy, on the Universally Lamented Death of the Incomparable Mr. Dryden* (1700), stanza 5, in Shawcross, *Critical Heritage*, p. 124.

8. See Shawcross, *Critical Heritage*, pp. 105–6 and 122–23.

9. See Thomas Newton's edition of *Paradise Regain'd. A Poem, in Four Books* [etc.]. *A New Edition, With Notes of various Authors* (London, 1752), pp. 3–4. On the other hand Warburton also reflected otherwise, with some reservation: "The *Paradise Regained* is a charming Poem; surely nothing inferior in the poetry and sentiment to the *Paradise Lost*; but, considered as a just composition in the Epic way, infinitely inferior; and indeed no more an Epic Poem than his 'Mansus.'"—Letter to Thomas Birch, dated 24 November 1737, printed in John Nichols, ed., *Illustrations of the Literary History of the Eighteenth Century* (London, 1817), vol. 2, pp. 77–82.

10. Quoted from Henry Crabbe Robinson's *Diary*, dated 7 January 1836, in Joseph A. Wittreich, *The Romantics on Milton* (Cleveland: The Press of Case Western Reserve University, 1970), p. 138.

manner, and refuted by the Son of God with strong unaffected eloquence, is the peculiar excellence of this Poem."[11]

Three important statements in the eighteenth century, ranging from 1711 to 1732 (and 1748) and 1779, ultimately argue for more objective readings of *Paradise Regain'd* and less emphasis on a comparison with *Paradise Lost*[12] and, by negative evidence, for readings without expectation of a standard religious interpretation of the way to regain paradise. The point is, of course, that even many who praise *Paradise Regain'd* for this or for that reason have clearly not read *Milton's* poem, have not understood his message, and have been interested in only versified orthodox dogma. The always astute Daniel Defoe, a great admirer of Milton, noting the superlatives directed toward *Paradise Lost*, observes: "The other is call'd a Dull Thing, infinitely short of the former, nothing to compare with it, and not like the same Author, and this is the Universal Opinion of the Age about these two Books: Mr. *Milton* was told this by several, for it was the opinion then as well as now [and we can add *and still now*], and his Answer was this—Well, I see the Reason plainly, why this Book is not liked so well as the other, for I am sure it is the better Poem of the two, but

11. John Jortin, *Remarks on Spenser's Poems* (1734), appendix on Milton, quoted in my *Milton 1732–1801: The Critical Heritage* (London: Routledge & Kegan Paul, 1972), pp. 87–88.

12. I must demur somewhat from Edward R. Weismiller's contention that "if the verse of *PR* deserves more attention in and for itself than it has thus far received, to fail to compare the verse of the two poems [*PR* and *PL*] would of course make no sense at all" ("Studies of Style and Verse Forms in *Paradise Regained*," *A Variorum Commentary on the Poems of John Milton* [New York: Columbia University Press, 1975], vol. 4: *Paradise Regained*, ed. Walter MacKellar, p. 253). While both fall under the rubric "blank verse" or, better, decasyllabic unrhymed verse, their bases are so different—*Paradise Lost* works in the verse paragraph with extensive enjambment and more intricate rhythms—that comparisons cannot be meaningful for either work. We do not need to consider dating and revision or the nature of what may have been revised—although some of the differences between the prosodies of the two poems may be accounted for thereby. What is significant, I think, is that the two poems are prosodically so different. Once bowing to "sense" and determining an overview of the prosodies of the two poems side by side, one has done enough and should then analyze the style and verse forms of each totally separately and without any further comparison or contrast: they are that different. Of course, Weismiller is here surveying the scholarship on the subject and so must engage such comparison.

People have not the same Gust of Pleasure at the regaining
Paradise, as they have concern at the loss of it, and therefore
they do not relish this so well as they did the other, tho' it be
without Comparison the best Performance."[13] The answer
Defoe puts into Milton's mouth also tells us something about
why we call *A Maske* "Comus" and why some think Satan the
hero of *Paradise Lost*.

The first published critical volume devoted exclusively to
just one poem of Milton's[14] was Richard Meadowcourt's *A
Critique on Milton's Paradise Regain'd* (London, 1732), slightly
amplified in its second edition, *A Critical Dissertation on Milton's
Paradise Regain'd* (London, 1748).[15] Meadowcourt opens his
critique thus: "The principal End of Poetry is Instruction,"
and he goes on to reflect further on poetry, occasioned, he
says, by an English poem. "The Reader will be surpriz'd at
hearing the Name of *Milton*'s *Paradise Regain'd*" as that poem,
however, for "Few Persons besides [Milton] have judg'd so
rightly of it." "The Verse of *Paradise Regain'd* is more artless
[than that of *Paradise Lost*], and is less embellish'd with Flights
of Imagination, and with Figures of Speech. But it supplies a
much richer Fund of intellectual Pleasure; it conveys the most
important Truths to the Understanding; it inspires the most
large and liberal Nations, and every where dissipates vulgar
Prejudices and popular Mistakes." The four chapters are
quite replete with quotations, which must have struck Mead-
owcourt as self-evident of the points he was making in his own
minimal discussion about the greatness of the poem. He does
add that "this invaluable Poem is not without Defects, and
that some slight Blemishes may be here and there discern'd";
these are in repetitions and "Similitudes and Allusions from
Romance and Fable," which create lessening effects. An an-

13. Daniel Defoe in *A Review of the State of the British Nation* 8, no. 63 (18 August
1711): 254–55, printed in Shawcross, *Critical Heritage*, p. 146.

14. Addison's *Spectator* papers were collected and published separately in 1719,
and Bernard Routh's *Lettres critiques a M. Le Comte ••• sur le Paradis Perdu, et Reconquis*
(Paris, 1731) is a 269-page examination of the two poems.

15. A facsimile edition of the 1732 printing by Joseph A. Wittreich was published
by Scholars' Facsimiles & Reprints (Gainesville, 1971). The volume also includes a
facsimile of Dunster's 1795 edition of the poem. Quotations are from pp. 1, 3 (2), 28.

swer to this "blemish" may be found in Annabel Patterson's essay previously noted.

The most voluble and influential critic during the eighteenth century, as everyone knows, was Samuel Johnson, and his negative epitomes of some of Milton's works or their alleged faults are often recited with varying intentions. But the paragraph on the brief epic in his "Life of Milton" has only sometimes been recalled, yet it is quite apt:

> Of *Paradise Regained*, the general judgement seems now to be right, that it is in many parts elegant, and every-where instructive. It was not to be supposed that the writer of *Paradise Lost* could ever write without great effusions of fancy, and exalted precepts of wisdom. The basis of *Paradise Regained* is narrow; a dialogue without action can never please like an union of the narrative and dramatick powers. Had this poem been written not by Milton, but by some imitator, it would have claimed and received universal praise.[16]

Modern critics would do well to heed these words: *elegant*, *instructive*; or their implications: minimal *effusion*, familiar *precepts of wisdom*; or their descriptions: *narrow*, *dialogue without action* as authorial intentions. The suggested separation from *Paradise Lost* comes through loud and clear. The poem should be read as it is, not as a reader thinks it should be, whether because it is Milton writing or because it deals with a subject religiously imbued.

These eighteenth-century views of Milton's "other" poem which we have been looking at have repeated themselves in the two ensuing centuries. The resumé of critical statements that Walter MacKellar distills in *A Variorum Commentary* attests to that repetition. There have been further egregious readings developed, like finding biographical elements in the poem

16. See Shawcross, *Critical Heritage 1732–1801*, p. 308.

(generally by those antagonistic to Milton as political person) or castigating the figure of Jesus (MacKellar consistently errs in calling him Christ!) as an artistic failure. One could do without such opacity. Indeed, I so often have a twinge as I read through the variorum commentary that it might be better to relegate all these obtuse studies to oblivion and not repeat them as if they deserved to be reckoned with at all. One thinks of Malcolm Ross's perverse views (based on his own religious and political persuasions, it is clear) in *Poetry and Dogma*,[17] which MacKellar dutifully had to recite as part of his obligation as variorum editor. Ross like others we have noted two and a half centuries before was bothered why Milton did not write a poem on the Crucifixion. As MacKellar tells us, C. S. Lewis answered that question—*twelve years before*: because he had more sense.[18]

An appropriate ending for these investigations of *Paradise Regain'd* that I am hopeful are cogent and will thereby prove meaningful to my reader is to quote Meadowcourt's last sentence about himself (pp. 29–30): "Tho' he is not conceited of his own Judgment, yet he wishes, in respect to what he has said of this neglected Poem, with which he confesses himself delighted, that the Readers may concur with him in the same Opinion, as he wishes they may share with him in the same Delight."

17. Malcolm Ross, *Poetry and Dogma* (New Brunswick: Rutgers University Press, 1954).

18. See *Variorum*, p. 18. Reference is to *A Preface to Paradise Lost* (London: Oxford University Press, 1942), p. 89.

Index

Addison, Joseph, 134, 136
Aeschylus, 30, 32, 34–35
Anonymous Biographer, 17–18
Aquinas, Saint Thomas, 113, 128
Aristotle, 120
Aubrey, John, 17

Baker, Stewart A., 96, 100
Barker, Arthur, 60
Barlow, Joel, 99
Bayle, Pierre, 132
Bible, 6. 29–30, 40, 42–43, 50, 52, 65,
    74–75, 89, 96, 112–13. Genesis,
    71–72. Exodus, 108; Exod. 3, 39;
    Exod. 17, 40. Deuteronomy 6, 40,
    42–43; 60; Deut. 8, 42–43. 1
    Samuel 14, 75. 1 Kings 9, 53.
    2 Kings 9–10, 29; 2 Kings 20, 74.
    1 Chronicles 21, 5. 2 Chronicles 32,
    74. Job, 5–7, 18, 87–88, 94, 97; Job
    1, 4–5, 87; Job 8, 16, 18; Job 18, 5.
    Psalms, 40, 50, 112; Psalm 2, 14,
    84–86, 89–91; Psalm 25, 64; Psalm
    91, 39, 86, 127; Psalm 109; 5; Psalm
    114, 71, 85–86. Proverbs 1 and 8,
    115. Zechariah 3, 5. Matthew, 50;
    Matt. 4, 39–40, 43, 65; Matt. 5, 1;
    Matt. 11, 64. Luke, 24, 50; Luke 4,
    39–40, 42–43; Luke 9, 125. John 1,
    65; John 7, 85; John 9, 74; John 13,
    2. 1 Corinthians 3, 16; 1 Cor. 6, 2.
    Philippians, 2, 2. 2 Peter 1, 44.
    1 John 3, 44. Revelation 4, 69.
biographical contexts, 9–28, 116–18
Bodleian Library, Catalogues, 15–16
Bradshaw, John, 20, 125
Browne, Sir Thomas, 105
Bush, Douglas, 104

Clarendon, Edward Hyde, Earl of, 117
Coleraine, Henry Hare, Baron, 16
covenant, 75, 88–89, 108–10
Crane, Hart, 6–7, 99
Cromwell, Oliver, 124–26
Cullen, Patrick, 45, 67, 106
Curran, Stuart A., 98, 106

Dante Alighieri, 2, 92
Defoe, Daniel, 135–36
Dennis, John, 131–32
Di Salvo, Jackie, 127–29
Dryden, John, 3, 111, 133
Dunster, Charles, 97–98, 136

Edwards, Jonathan, 108
Egan, James, 108
Ellwood, Thomas, 3, 12–15, 25, 34,
    74, 102, 114, 128, 133
Erasmus, Desiderius, 120
Erikson, Erik H., 62–63
Euripides, 30
Evans, J. M., 43

Fairfax, Sir Thomas, 123–25
Faustus, 50
Fisch, Harold, 5
Fish, Stanley, 78
Fletcher, Harris F., 13, 18, 77
Freud, Sigmund, 53, 66

Gilbert, Allan, H., 32
Griffin, Dustin, 132
Guss, Donald L., 95–96, 100

Hamilton, Gary D., 61
Heimbach, Peter, 21
Hill, Christopher, 117, 124–26
Hobbes, Thomas, 116, 118, 126–27
Homer, 92–93, 132
Hunter, William B., 33
Hyde, Thomas, 15–16

Johnson, Samuel, 137
Jordan, Richard D., 105
Jortin, John, 134–35
Joyce, James, 67
Jung, Carl, 2, 6–7, 68, 128

Kantra, Robert A., 83–84
Key to Paradise, The, 16

139